NATURAL HEALTH

NATURAL HEALTH FOR THE ELDERLY

How to Maintain Happiness and
Vitality in the Later Years

by

ALAN MOYLE
N.D., M.B.N.O.A.

THORSONS PUBLISHERS LIMITED
Wellingborough, Northamptonshire

First published 1975

ISBN 0 7225 0303 2

Filmset by
Specialised Offset Services Ltd., Liverpool
and printed in Great Britain by
Whitstable Litho Ltd., Whitstable, Kent

CONTENTS

CHAPTER ONE

THE AGEING POPULATION

In an era of pollution, grim forecasts of dwindling natural resources and expanding world population, the rich developed countries have to add another problem – age. People are living longer. In Great Britain alone, the average age of the population has doubled in 150 years. Over half the male population of Britain achieves 70 years of age, while half the females reach 75.

The number of elderly people increases every year and, according to present trends, is likely to do so for the next 40 to 50 years. It is estimated that 11 per cent of the British people are over 65 years of age.

Broad evidence of an ageing population is seen in most districts. Certain areas, however, are especially favoured by the elderly, since they tend, whenever economic circumstances permit, to migrate to a warmer and more equable climate. South-coast towns have a preponderance of elderly residents. The 1971 census shows Bexhill-on-Sea, Sussex, having 12,425 people born before 1905 out of a total population of 32,849. Similar, but not so high returns, were made for other East Sussex coastal towns. In that census, Hastings – with a population of 72,170 as a whole – had 17,670 people of 65 and over.

'Geriatrica' Districts

Unequal distribution of elderly people raises special problems. Seaside towns favoured by the elderly will require more and more from the health and social services of the country. Warnings about avoiding 'geriatrica' districts for retirement have some logic. The advantages of sunnier skies, cleaner air and a warmer climate, however, are very difficult to forego. It is inevitable, therefore, that the age drift to a more equable environment will continue. Local authorities with a geriatric problem can obviously present a solid case for increased financial assistance from national funds to meet that problem.

Unfortunately, the problem is not solved by money alone. Older people require care, and care means skilled people to minister to the older population. Staffing is one of the largest problems of the public and private institutions catering for the aged. Nor is it always because such staff are too frequently underpaid. Unsocial hours and the very nature of the work deter many from devoting themselves to the care of the elderly and infirm. The problem is only brought home to people when they have to try and make arrangements – even if temporary – for an elderly person to be placed somewhere for care and attention.

Private institutions – often grossly understaffed – are usually beyond the financial means of the ordinary person. This means that more and more home care is required. On the whole, providing that this can be backed up by sufficient outside assistance, financial, social and medical, home care is the happiest and most humane solution to the problems of the elderly.

Problems of Adjustment

Large numbers of elderly British venture even further – principally to the Mediterranean scene. Warmth and reduced taxation are absorbing problems for the elderly. The same problem arises in the northern European countries, Canada and the northern states of America. But retirement centres, whether in Spain, Portugal, North Africa, Florida or elsewhere, can cause problems to people who do not easily adjust.

The advantages and disadvantages of a purely ageing community have to be carefully considered, even when that community is relatively free from financial worry. Mature people should think twice before seeking comparative freedom from the rough and tumble of life. To be alive and feel alive also demands a certain amount of friction and irritation. It also demands contact and communication with all ages. Security and a sense of being wanted are also problems of this group. Moving can be a heart-rending decision. It is a decision which is best faced before or shortly after retirement and then only after much deliberation.

Delaying decisions about what to do in the latter part of life is a common habit. Thought which should be applied at 50 is often delayed until 60 or even 70. It is a natural instinct to dismiss notions about retirement or ageing. The prospect has to be faced by all at some time or other, but at 50 or 60 there is an understandable but misguided aversion to making plans for retirement and old age. Yet few people fail to plan by insurance. Indeed, hundreds of thousands are now assured of higher pensions because of their employment.

One of the inconsistencies of people is that they will insure for accidents, disease and death and yet do little about health. Insurance companies advertise extensively and have a persuasive influence. Private and national insurance schemes cover all manner of contingencies. Unfortunately, however, they are mainly concentrated on pensions, disease and death.

People are not only going to live longer, they are steadily becoming conditioned to the fact. The awareness of a longer life-span is possibly one of the reasons for the growth in insurance. That the nation will have to support a steadily increasing proportion of pensioners is an accepted fact. More and more resources will have to be devoted to care for the aged. What is unfortunate is that too many of these resources are, and will be, allocated to necessary but negative ends.

There are obvious reasons for a lengthening of the life-span. Prominent amongst these are improved social and economic conditions, the eradication of many infectious diseases due to increased knowledge and better hygiene, technological improvements – not least in surgery – and 'life-saving' drugs! More and more people are kept alive – or half alive – by advances in surgery and the 'wonder' drugs.

A Menace to Health

In general it must be admitted that toxic drugs, with their familiar dangerous side-effects, constitute a menace to health. Drugs, especially pain-killing and sleeping drugs, are used indiscriminately by the general public, despite repeated warnings. It is these very drugs which, by sapping energy and reducing resistance to disease, not only limit the value of drugs should they be necessary in later life, but accelerate the degeneration in physical well-being.

Many lives are saved by cortico-steroid and other drugs which, despite their toxic nature, have a place in a humane society. It is not sufficient to declare that all drugs are dangerous. When human resistance to pain or disease is at a very low ebb, then all available means must be taken to assist recovery, even when the side-effects of such means must be taken into account. What is to be deplored, however, is the indiscriminate use of drugs which poison the system and cause unnecessary and early degeneration.

There is no doubt that life can be prolonged by potent drugs. But is that sufficient? The vitally important factor in ageing is degeneration. Degeneration can be delayed and reduced, adding many *active* years of life. Chronological age is of little significance if life holds no flavour. To be a 'cabbage' at 70, 80 or 90 is not an enjoyable prospect. Even worse is the thought of being crippled and confined by the degenerative processes of ageing.

Adding active years to life is the biggest challenge of our time. It is a challenge which can immeasurably increase the productivity and happiness of millions of people and reduce the cost of social services. Preventing, delaying, reducing and minimizing the effects of degenerative disease, therefore, is the most important factor in the ageing process.

Life imposes many stresses and strains. Some are inevitable and most people are equipped with sufficient mental and physical resources to deal with the normal hazards of life. Accidents and disease can alter the pattern of ageing for the worse. Even so, the human system is normally endowed with resilience and immense recuperative powers – even in the latter part of life.

A Gradual Process
Life, like evolution, is governed by 'the inevitability of gradualness'. In the normal adult age does not come on overnight. Age and disease have a great deal in common in that both are accelerated by accidents, abuse, stress, environment and disregard of natural laws in nutrition. The same aggravation and deficiencies in diet and normal care of the body which cause rheumatism, constipation, catarrh and coronaries cause the 'ageing' of cells which determines the *active* life span of the body.

It is a personal and social responsibility to maintain active health. Only by doing so can sufficient resources be allocated to the less fortunate members of the elderly population. Life can never be equal, it can never be free from accidents or misfortunes. No one can be sure they will never need aid. The aim, therefore, should be to reduce the possibilities and extent of such aid by keeping physically fit.

Luck and environment have a part in the causation of early ageing. But there is no replacement for self-discipline, moderation and intelligent nutrition in helping to ensure that the degeneration of age does not set in too early or too severely. The warning signs of the thirties must be obeyed. When the midriff begins to thicken, movements slow down and vague pains begin to assert themselves – that is the time to take stock. *Days can be long, but years fly by.*

CHAPTER TWO

DELAYING DEGENERATION

Degenerative diseases are the predominant feature in ageing. These same diseases, however, are amongst those most influenced, for better or worse, by past history. Apart from unavoidable accidents, unsought mental and physical stresses of an exceptional nature and other similar quirks in life, a healthy old age is well within the reach of everyone. Health is a personal endowment and a personal responsibility.

Health in children is the responsibility of parents. In youth and early life it is take for granted. It is still often being taken for granted, and abused, at 45. Yet more often than not the seeds of degeneration have been sown at 35 or earlier. Even when there has been no actual physical injury or illness of sufficient importance to leave scarring, neglect of simple health rules and faulty nutrition have damaged future health. Obesity, for instance, reduces the expectation of life and accelerates degenerative disease. It is calculated that to be 25 lbs overweight at 45 reduces expectation of life by 25 per cent.

Harmful Indulgences
Obesity is, in the main, a sign of indulgence. It is, however, far from being the only indulgence. There are many more which set the seal on early degeneration. Lack of exercise – television alone has created a vast captive and inactive section of the population – has a pampering and debilitating effect. Private transport and even power tools and other labour-saving devices, can also be a menace. Civilized communities can hardly forego such amenities, but they should never totally exclude some physical effort. Smoking is a harmful indulgence, so is excessive drinking of alcohol, tea, or coffee. Any or all of these indulgences can cause impotence in early middle age. The prospect of early impotence should not be lightly dismissed, since it entails possibilities of marital disharmony. It is too easy to be pampered and soft.

Age means change. Ageing commences at birth and ends in death. In the interval, however, is the life-span which is punctuated by countless hazards, experiences and, only too frequently, misfortunes. Environment and nutrition vary from person to person, in the same manner that their experiences differ. The older one becomes the more vicissitudes one has had to suffer, and the misfortunes and misdemeanours of the *previous years* have a great influence on ageing.

With so many anomalies it is impossible to define the chronological age. One man can be 'geriatric' at 60 and another not until 80 or 90. A geriatric person is not necessarily a senile person. It would, in fact, be probably much better if the term 'geriatric' was clearly reserved for the type of person, mobile or immobile, who retained full mental powers but whose physical activity, reflexes and natural functions demonstrated the inevitable effects of ageing.

One of the merciful aspects of real senility is that the senile person is largely or even totally unaware of the indignity of complete physical or mental collapse. The great burden is on those immediately responsible for that person. Thousands of older people who require some assistance or guidance, are very sensitive on this issue and can be irrationally independent from fear of being classed as senile or semi-senile. There is nothing wrong in ageing; it comes to all. But it has to be recognized. People are living longer and the ageing section of the population enlarges every year.

Premature Ageing

That ageing should vary from person to person is easily understood. A few fortunate people go through life well-nourished, free from serious illnesses, relatively immune to mental or physical trauma and happier and more contented than the average. But life is not equal. Nutritional disorders – either from existing on cheap 'filling' foods with vitamin and mineral deficiencies or over-indulgence – can equally ensure premature ageing.

Accidents, even when recovery seems complete, leave scarring which is a later disadvantage. Many a football or rugby knee is a later focal point for arthritis. Trauma, whether mental or physical, sets its mark on future years. Severe illnesses impose the same drain on natural resources. Lack of discipline over mind and body in youth becomes a disadvantage in later years. Lack of exercise or the other extreme – severe exhaustion – both impose penalties for which account has to be made some time.

Obviously, the more accidents, stresses or vicissitudes there are in life, the earlier some physical decline is going to be reached. What must not be overlooked, however, is the remarkable healing powers which nature embodies in the human make-up. The inherent healing powers of the body overcome many an ailment. Frequently nature heals, despite orthodox drug therapy.

The naturopathic contention is that the body, when diseased, must be treated as a whole and that therapy should be aimed at encouraging the vital forces of the body to cure the ailment. The failure of orthodox medicine is that it treats – or even suppresses – the disease and does little to seek the real cause of the disease. Toxic drugs which may suppress or relieve one ailment usually have side-effects which create other man-made diseases.

There is no doubt that toxic drugs – even many so-called harmless medicines or tablets – have side-effects which damage the tissues and hasten the onset of degenerative changes. Avoiding drugs can add years to active and productive life and counter degenerative changes.

It is an established fact that, when a person is hospitalized, he or she is more prone to infection. Furthermore, hospitals are increasingly filled with cases who are actually suffering from drug poisoning or the long-term side-effects of common drugs. These ailments can range from liver and kidney diseases, internal haemorrhages, gastric diseases to degeneration of the nervous system.

The other plus factor, however, is that, where the body cannot completely heal – and most damage leaves some scarring – it can compensate. Compensation is not perfection, but a higher standard of general health raises the degree of complete recovery or compensation.

Correct and balanced nutrition, sound habits, exercise and self-discipline play a large part in delaying older age. Once reached, however, it is necessary to adapt. The process is gradual but it does infer a change in nutrition, outlook and physical effort.

Blood Circulation

At the more advanced level of age the blood circulation slows down and the metabolic rate drops. The fact that arteries harden and the smaller blood vessels tend to become more constricted is an impediment to blood circulation. Reduced mobility in the spine and joints causes local tension, difficulty in breathing, congestion and interference with the flow of blood and nerve impulses. The blood carries nutriment and oxygen to the tissues and transports waste products and CO_2 back to the organs of elimination. Any impediment to blood circulation, therefore, creates nutritional imbalance, lack of oxygen and an accumulation of waste products in the bloodstream.

Reduced or delayed accommodation to positional changes because of interference with the blood supply to the brain is a frequent cause of loss of balance. Balance can be a profound worry to elderly people, since falls are a major cause of serious accidents, burns and fractures. Degeneration in the joints, arteries and neuro-muscular system is less bearable when it creates difficulties in balance, since it adds anxieties and creates lack of confidence. Falls, which play a minor part in younger life, are more serious in age, when bones are fragile. It is estimated that over 70 per cent of fatal accidents in the home involve people of 65 and over, with falls as the largest cause of mortality.

In the aged the quality of the blood is vital. An increased flow of blood is not accommodated so easily in the elderly. It is, therefore, essential that the blood carried should be of the highest possible quality. Reduced haemoglobin content of the blood as a result of nutritional deficiencies and impairment of haematosis (formation into blood) is a common form of anaemia in the older person.

The reduction in accommodation is also complicated by a reduction in absorption and assimilation. This means that extra care has to be taken to ensure that deficiencies in diet are avoided.

The reduced physical activity and metabolic rate of the ageing means that calorie requirements are correspondingly less. The cheap 'filling' foods – especially white flour and white sugar products – should be avoided by all, but more so as age progresses. There is, or should be, a natural reduction in appetite of the aged; therefore, to maintain an efficient alkaline balance and to ensure an adequate supply of vitamins and mineral salts, diet assumes significant importance. Less food should be consumed, and preferably at more frequent intervals. The diet should also contain less 'filling' foods and more vitamin and mineral rich items in an easily digested form. In age, for instance, calcium absorption is frequently impaired, leading to osteoporosis and fragile bones. Additional calcium in the diet is required to avoid this. Because absorption and assimilation is imperfect in age, nutritional deficiencies can arise, even when the diet is balanced.

Correct nutrition and the prevention or reduction of the degenerative diseases are vital to health in later years. What is not sufficiently recognized is that the future is governed by the past. The foundation of sound health in the latter part of life is laid in the early and middle years. 'What ye sow, so shall ye reap' is a very apt quotation.

Condition Determines Age

Ageing, as we have seen, however, is an extremely variable factor. What is not variable is the necessity to maintain health throughout life and limit degeneration to an acceptable level, even in the very last stages. Age is a matter of condition, not years. Under normal circumstances and given reasonable luck, mental and physical activity can be maintained up to, or almost up to, the very end of life. This is well within the bounds of possibility when the problems of degenerative diseases are recognized and preventative measures are adopted, before it is too late.

In the following chapters it is proposed to discuss methods of preventing or mitigating the degenerative diseases so common in later life. Nutrition, with special reference to the elderly, will first come under review. This subject is of profound importance. It is just as damaging to be over-fed as under-fed. The quality of blood and its circulation depend upon correct diet. It is imbalance in diet which lowers resistance to disease. This, in turn, produces many of the common ailments which are frequently nature's attempt to cleanse the system and redress the imbalance.

The foundation of chronic ailments is made by ignoring nature's warnings and suppressing minor ailments by the use of toxic drugs. If the dietetic and other errors continue, then stronger drugs are used to suppress or alleviate the symptoms. One misconception leads to another, but the end-result is frequently a crippling chronic complaint which marks an early degeneration.

Age brings its own peculiar hazards and pitfalls and these will also be discussed, as well as the problems of retirement. What must not be overlooked, however, is the fact that age is a matter of feeling and condition. It is also a matter of personal responsibility which should not be abdicated.

Prevention of Degenerative Disease

With the ever-increasing cost of social services and institutional care, together with the demand on available manpower and resources, it is imperative that more and more importance should be attached to the prevention and reduction of degenerative diseases. It is these diseases which tax the social services and are a cause of social distress and frustration. Prevention, therefore, should rank as equal or even more important than the treatment of degenerative disease.

It is a reflection on intelligence that more attention is paid to dealing with a health problem than is given to avoiding that problem. It is like waiting for a situation to arise, knowing it will arise, before doing anything about it. When a car is going down a very steep gradient the prudent driver engages a lower gear or gives an occasional touch to the brake; he does not wait till the last moment to take evasive action. Yet people will wait till it is either too late or almost too late to do anything about the degenerative diseases which will hamper them in later life.

Nature flashes the warnings and applies the brakes. Pain is an indication of malaise and a warning sign. When it is not suppressed by drugs, the brakes are applied. Practically all illnesses are acute ailments when they first appear in the body. Colds, catarrh, fevers, diarrhoea and the first twinges of rheumatism are, like headaches and nausea, acute reactions. In acute ailments the body tends to reject poisons that have been absorbed or accumulated within the system – as in the case of food poisoning. Diarrhoea, nausea and vomiting meet the need. In colds and catarrh the body is trying to throw off excess mucus caused by either chemical or toxic irritation of the mucous membranes (fumes, tobacco, dust, etc.), or because of an excess of mucus-forming food in the diet. Headaches can arise from a variety of factors, including lack of oxygen, constipation and stress. The first twinges of rheumatism, low back pain or lumbago usually arise from a combination of excessive acidity and poor posture.

To suppress the pains of acute ailments by the use of drugs is the first mistake. On the surface it may seem attractive and logical to kill the pain. But killing pain, which is merely a warning, does not remove the cause. Furthermore, the drugs used add to the toxic elements circulating in the bloodstream.

Repeated suppression of acute ailments is the largest cause of chronic disease. It is also illogical in the sense that the mistakes which caused the pain are repeated again and again.

Ancient Greek and biblical teaching assumed that the body changed every seven years. Puberty came at 14, manhood at 21, the climacteric (in women) at 42 and the life-span was 70. To some extent this is still true.

There is, however, another factor in life which some experts have called 'the 20-year-rule'. This law or rule applies to the time it takes for the body to feel the full effects of unnatural environment and imbalanced nutrition in manifestations of disease in the body. This '20-year-rule' can only be average. Addiction to common drugs, especially the excessive use of pain-killers, tranquillizers, sleeping pills and antacid concoctions would shorten that period. Excessive stress would also have an unfavourable influence.

CHAPTER THREE

THE AGEING PROCESS

Ageing is a continuous process varying, not only from person to person, but in differing aspects in the same individual. This explains why some old people can be physically healthy, but with an irritatingly old and defective memory. Others, crippled with arthritis or some other degenerative disease, retain a decisive and clear-cut intellect. One part of the body, in effect, may age more rapidly than another.

The rate of ageing, of course, entirely depends upon nutrition, environment, freedom from disease, undue stress and serious accidents. The saying 'creaking gates last longer' is only true when the long-term ailment does not seriously attack the vital organs and the patient is cushioned against stress, and other hazards, in a protective environment. In such cases, too, there has usually been ample time to adapt.

The physical signs of old age or normal senescence are obvious. Even when the erect posture is maintained there is a loss of height because changes in the spine produce a shrinkage of the intervertebral discs. Normally, however, the height loss is accentuated by the posture of general flexion characterized by the forward droop of the head, the stooping spine and partially bent knees.

Ageing Skin

The skin of an old person is drier, flabby and inelastic. The gradual loss of subcutaneous fat and sebaceous secretion is a further indication of an ageing skin. Wrinkles are an obvious result of the above. The question of how and when degeneration of the skin will appear depends a great deal upon previous nutrition, health and care of the skin. In normal senescence, however, discoloration and dehydration of the skin are fairly common. What are a great worry to many old people are the seborrhoeic warts which frequently appear on the trunk – and sometimes on the face and scalp. Such warts are rarely malignant, though checks should always be made.

In age the bones lighten, lose some elasticity and become porous. Some bones, like the mandible, for instance, tend to change shape. Distortion of the neck of the femur increases shearing stresses and increases the danger of fracture of that bone. Normal weight-bearing stress also distorts bones, especially in the obese person with a poor posture. Kyphosis and scoliosis of the spine can often be traced as much to postural defects and defective chest expansion as to actual bone changes. Frequently it is a combination of both factors. Calcification of cartilages and ligaments is often normal in age and muscles lose bulk and strength.

Movement in the elderly is slower and less definite because of the degenerative changes in bones, muscles, ligaments and cartilage. Alongside, however, are the changes in the nervous system which also affect movement. Quick voluntary movements become more difficult to perform through a decrease in co-ordination. The complete neuro-muscular mechanism suffers in age. This is often demonstrated in the failure or slowness to make corrective movements when taken off-balance.

Loss of Balance
It is necessary to understand and appreciate the hesitancy of the elderly in movement, since a loss of balance can so easily culminate in a fall and a fractured bone. One such fall, or the threat of it, undermines confidence. Movement, however, is as vital to the aged person as to the young. Even in the elderly, muscle power and bulk can be restored to some extent. Stagnation, congestion and further limitation of movement can arise from too much rest. The safety of a chair or bed can be very tempting for many old people, but the necessity for physical activity must take precedence over safety. Skin sores and even permanent contractures can arise from too much bed rest.

Age produces marked changes in the nervous system, making reflexes slower and generally affecting muscle tone. The main cellular units in the nervous system do not reproduce like other cells. With cells in the brain dying at an increasing speed in later age, memory, reflexes and co-ordination suffer. The loss of cells in the brain does not mean that intellect suffers, but taste, smell and tactile discrimination are normally impaired. Pain is the least affected of the senses. The pain threshold varies in all individuals right from birth. That pain may be felt more in age than in earlier life could be due to the increased anxiety and half-expectancy of pain some older people acquire.

Sight and hearing are so frequently impaired in age that it

tends to be accepted as normal. Many old people, however, have but slight loss of vision or hearing. Mechanical aids in spectacles and hearing aids do reduce the physical inconvenience of defective sight or hearing, providing they are correctly fitted and periodically checked for accuracy. (For those with impaired vision large-print books are available, both from bookshops and libraries.) The retention of both senses to a really advanced age is possible when past history is good. The gradual loss of visual field can be delayed by moderation in the smoking and alcohol habits and the maintenance of basic nutritional levels. Smell is another sense which diminishes with age. Catarrh, which can be avoided by correct nutrition and care, is responsible for a great deal of deafness and loss of smell.

There are many factors which adversely affect balance in the more mature person. Sight, hearing, posture, slow reflexes, arterio-sclerosis, hypertension, middle-ear disease, lack of confidence and diseases affecting movement (rheumatism and arthritis), all contribute to loss of balance and mobility. One important factor, however, is often overlooked; care of the feet. Chiropody is widely available, even to the aged. The feet, however, particularly women's feet, are often distorted in earlier years. Oedema of the feet and ankles, allied to bunions, corns and tender pressure points is an obvious impediment to movement. Painful and swollen feet are a powerful consideration to an older person already worried about balance. Many older people use the excuse of painful feet to escape the effort of movement. This is unwise, since long periods of immobility produce stagnation, further oedema and decreased confidence and mobility.

Lung Capacity
Even without disease the normal ventilatory capacity of the lungs diminishes with age. Residual air, namely the air remaining in the lungs after maximum expiration, increases with age. Maximum expiration and inspiration decreases. Reduction in lung capacity and performance means that total ventilatory effort must increase to produce the same amount of energy previously put out in younger years. Age produces a gradual dilatation of the air space in the lungs. The reduction in muscle power and decrease in thoracic mobility consequent upon ageing, together with dilatation of the air spaces, means that breathlessness on effort can be a common condition in age.

Dyspnoea (distress in breathing) therefore, is not necessarily a sign of disease, it can be just symptomatic of age. This degenerative symptom can be held at bay by moderation in living, the maintenance of mobility, muscular power and good posture. Postural defects – such as habitual stooping – should be corrected at as early an age as possible to avoid inevitable damage to the shape and mobility of the thoracic cage.

Absorption and assimilation of food is less efficient as the years go by. Gastric mobility is reduced and active peristalsis, the mechanism by which the gastric contents are propelled through the gastro-intestinal tract, has briefer periods of activity. In the older person there is lessened sugar tolerance and a reduction in the quantity of gastric juice. Hydrochloric acid deficiency may arise, partly because of atrophy of the glandular elements of the stomach and possibly because of a deficiency of the Vitamin B-complex, iron and calcium. The necessity for sound nutrition, therefore, is always stressed.

The digestion of food begins in the mouth and it is essential that older people should not neglect their teeth. Even when dentures or partial dentures are worn, these must be checked at intervals to ensure that mastication is at as high a standard as possible. Sore gums from badly-fitting dentures can interfere with mastication and cause unnecessary pain and discomfort.

Although the ageing heart is less capable of exerting extra effort, it can, when necessary, enlarge providing the increase in bulk is a gradual process. The heart valves tend to become more rigid with age. The heart itself is dependent upon nutritional factors. Fibrosis of the muscle tissue of the heart is often due, not to ageing, but to nutritional deficiencies which affect the arterial system and, ultimately, the heart tissue. The dangers of excessive animal fat consumption, salt, white sugar and white flour products must be fully appreciated.

Calcification of Arteries

Arteries, which also depend upon sound nutrition and a good environment, tend to become less elastic and have some degree of calcification (hardening) in age. Such changes cause an increase in blood-pressure which can be assumed to be normal as age increases. This same change is seen in the arteries generally, though it is often difficult to differentiate between when degeneration is caused by disease conditions and what would arise normally from ageing. Calcification of the aorta and the peripheral blood vessels is common in age, but since there is a corresponding reduction in physical effort, it can still be synonymous with health. Degenerative changes in the walls of the arteries cause the pulse wave to have a more rapid propagation. This is one explanation for the increased pulse-pressure and trend towards higher systolic blood-pressures in age. Spinal and arterial mobility are all-important aspects in ageing.

One of the differences between the elderly and the normal child or adult is the reaction to acute disease where fever is a predominant symptom. Little is yet known about the failure or decline of the heat regulating mechanism in elderly people. Certainly less body heat is spontaneously generated, because of limitation or lack of movement. Many old people have a normal temperature of around 95°F. or 35°C. This temperature would cause shivering, vaso-constriction, pulse and blood-pressure rise and diuresis in younger people. But old people who are prone to hypothermia (sub-normal temperature) fail to shiver and vaso-constrict sufficiently. Even in normal people of advancing years this vital response to cold loses its efficiency. The lack of a fever reaction can be a hindrance to recovery.

Symptoms of Hypothermia
Hypothermia is more of a danger in the winter and is said to be aggravated by the habitual use of barbiturates and other sedatives and tranquillizers. With present drug-taking tendencies, this malfunction of the heat-regulating mechanism is bound to increase as the years slip by. Hypothermia is a very dangerous state, demanding the most urgent attention with careful and slow re-heating of the body. Heat must never be applied too quickly to the hypothermic patient. Slow rewarming spontaneously under a blanket in a warm room is usually necessary, with the heat in the room being gradually raised at about 1°F. per hour. Hypothermia is recognized by muscle rigidity, clouded consciousness, slow speech, pale skin and by the cold feel of the skin of the protected parts, namely the abdomen and inner parts of the thighs.

Hypothermia can be avoided in age by retaining mobility, sound nutrition and adequate warmth. Excessive use of alcohol is also implicated in hypothermia, so moderation in alcohol and avoidance of drugs is a safeguard. Tight and heavy clothing is not the answer. Light but warm clothes and sufficient heat and movement are essential to avoid a condition which, under normal circumstances, should rarely arise.

Combination of Degenerative Changes

Posture, diseases of the joints, neuro-muscular degeneration, hypertension, and arterio-sclerosis are frequently connected, one factor impinging upon the other, all contributing to a general decline in balance and mobility. The general picture, which tends to become accepted as normal in advancing years, in fact is not one of disease, but of a combination of several degenerative changes, each varying in intensity from time to time and from person to person. This is in contrast to younger age groups, where one particular ailment, with its side-effects, is the normal state of affairs.

In age, adverse influences have wider implications and impose more of a threat to health. On the other hand, the recovery rate tends to be underestimated. Older people can and do recover from acute ailments with almost the same speed as younger people. The fact that, in age, when normal resistance is possibly lower, this achievement is assisted by modern drugs, makes no difference to the end result. The drugs are stopped when normal health has returned and the side-effects of the drugs can be eliminated in time. It has been previously mentioned that the essentials for recovery, even when surgery is necessary, is previous sound nutrition, a clean bloodstream and maximum mobility.

The common degenerative diseases are those which attack the nervous system, arterial diseases, the locomotor system and the respiratory function. Many of the problems connected with the degenerative diseases are either avoidable or capable of being minimized by preventative methods in earlier years. For a person to reach an advanced age at all implies a certain degree of virility, care, good hereditary influences and freedom from severe accidents or malignancy.

Reflex Failure

Degeneration in the nervous system is demonstrated in older people by slower reflexes, faulty memory, changes in sight, touch, hearing, smell and taste. Reflexes which in normal adult people can be used as diagnostic aids are not so reliable in the elderly. Between the ages of 70 and 90 several reflexes can be lost without any significant change in health. What has to be accepted is that, in age, certain 'abnormalities' in the nervous system are normal for that age. The same law can apply to the circulatory system and most functions of the body. What is always evident is the inter-dependence of one particular system on another. Health is a total matter, the body being a complete unit. Despite the fact that one part of the body may age quicker than another, an acceptable level of health can be maintained in advanced years because of the total diminution in activity and demands upon the body.

What is common in age is that many of the so-called neurological disorders are the outcome of other degenerative changes ranging from diseased joints, changes in the spine, obstruction to the blood flow and poor posture. Nutritional deficiencies are also a common contributory cause of nerve degeneration. A stroke is an example of a vascular condition bringing about drastic changes in the nervous function of the affected part of the body. Changes in the spine from disc degeneration, bone disease or bad posture, can cause interference with the nerve supply, the interference varying with the site of the lesion in the spine.

Apart from correct nutrition, what has not yet been adequately recognized is the important role manipulative therapy can play in maintaining mobility, muscular power, ventilatory efficiency, a free blood flow and an unobstructed nerve supply. Nervous degeneration is an important factor in age. Its rate depends on the health of the body as a whole. Corrective measures are available. Such measures should not be limited to the occasional manipulation for sciatica, lumbago or a stiff joint.

The neglect of anatomical disturbance, or lack of mobility in the spine is a frequent cause of early degeneration in the spine and nerve function. Adaptation or compensation will often take place, but the weakness will persist to some degree or other and become manifest in later life. Past history influences future health and this is very true when the derangement in the nervous system can be traced to a fault or faults in the spinal mechanics or in postural defects.

Spinal Defects

Spinal integrity has an all-important influence on the nervous system. Injuries or abnormalities which are neglected hasten the degeneration of vertebrae, the inter-vertebral discs and the nerves issuing from the lesioned area. Reflex disturbances arising from the lesion area create muscle tension and interfere with the blood supply and nutrition to the part involved.

Paraplegia (paralysis of the lower extremities) may have a vascular cause, arising from a history of two or more separate strokes, paralysis developing on one side previous to the other. But paraplegia is more frequently due to compression of the spinal cord. In younger people this compression is most likely to be due to accidents. But in older people compression of the spinal cord can arise from cervical spondylosis, degeneration or protrusion of intervertebral discs or from bone disease such as osteoporosis. The latter are both degenerative diseases in which manipulative therapy is contra-indicated.

Cervical spondylosis and osteoporosis will be discussed under arthritis and rheumatism, but it must be emphasized that neither is an inevitable result of ageing.

The picture of advancing years need not be so frightening as appears. In the first place, a great number of the disadvantages of age are avoidable. Even when accidents and stress have taken their toll, compensation and adaptation can reduce their effects. Competition and ambition lose their disturbing elements and an increased tolerance and acceptance of life often produce a more tranquil mental attitude.

The fears of insecurity, loneliness, accidents and illness are real. Such fears are best brought into the open and faced. Problems for the senior citizen do exist. No one can pretend otherwise. Enlarging the problems, for selfish reasons of gaining sympathy, is not unknown. To a certain extent dependence upon others is inevitable in later life. The degree of this dependence and the age at which it commences is, by and large, in the hands of each individual. Physical age and chronological age are two different things.

A great deal depends upon the environment and upon the nutritional and other factors mentioned. A great deal more, however, depends upon the individual's approach. Discipline, a positive mental attitude and a determination to retain as much mobility as possible is essential. But health should be a goal, not an obsession.

CHAPTER FOUR

NUTRITION

The word 'diet' is anathema to millions of people. It has come to be connected with discipline in eating or with the necessity to lose weight. Nutrition, on the other hand, has connotations of either massive hunger or a sub-standard level of feeding associated with natural disasters or war in undeveloped countries. It is unfortunate that nutrition, in its narrow sense, is based on calorie levels. A calorie is a standard unit of heat. Its main purpose is to estimate the physiological values of differing food materials according to the amount of heat they produce on being oxidized in the body. Calories, however, are only a part of nutrition.

Errors in nutrition, either by over-feeding or under-feeding, influence premature ageing. One of the characteristics of really old and healthy people is usually moderation in all things. This moderation has, more often than not, covered a long life span of a frugal or even monotonous diet. On examination, however, the diet has contained all the necessary ingredients for maintaining health without taxing the gastro-intestinal system. Food, in effect, had been used with the maximum economy and efficiency to nurture cells and promote growth and activity.

Nutritional 'Disasters'

Two nutritional 'disasters' which undermine the health and vigour of the developed areas of the world are white flour and white sugar, and all articles of food which have both or one of these items as main ingredients. This covers a vast number of food products, ranging from white bread and pastries down to chocolates, sweets and sweet drinks. If such items were only used sparingly, the position would not be so alarming. Unfortunately, however, the evidence proves otherwise. The bulk of the nation, and not just this nation, appears determined to condemn itself to a policy of being 'half-alive'.

White sugar and white flour have long been condemned as a menace to health. In their natural state of sugar cane, beet, and wholewheat, it would be physically impossible to over-eat either. But in the refined and concentrated forms in which they appear

– especially sugar – it is very easy to consume too much of both. For instance, it requires 2½lbs of sugar beet to supply 5oz of sugar. That amount is the average daily sugar consumption per head. A normal-sized apple contains about a heaped teaspoonful of natural sugar.

Young and physically active individuals can offset a great number of dietetic errors by exercise and involvement in outdoor activities. From about 25 on, however, too many people begin to shirk actual physical effort and spend less time in the open air. At 35, this factor is even more pronounced.

Refined Carbohydrates

As the years progress and the consumption of refined carbohydrates persist, a decline in health and resistance to disease becomes more apparent. People, in effect, become old before their time in most sophisticated countries. It is essential to reverse the process before too many years have passed.

In young and early life colds, catarrh, fevers and other acute ailments are frequent manifestations of the body's attempt to eliminate toxic material accumulated in the system. Even acne in teenagers demonstrates the way the skin – one of the organs of elimination – is being used to expel morbid matter. It is suppression of these early symptoms of disease or imbalance, and the continuation of their causes, that leads to chronic disease and early degeneration.

Acute catarrh, more often than not, is due to an excess of refined carbohydrates. Unfortunately, refined carbohydrates are only part, admittedly a large part, of the errors in nutrition which lead to early degeneration. The excessive use of fats, particularly processed fats, is known to be implicated in the cardio-vascular disorders like coronary thrombosis and arterio-sclerosis.

Cholesterol Increase

High cholesterol levels in the blood are due to an excess of saturated fats, plus an over-consumption of butter, milk, cream, cheese and eggs. Eggs, especially those from battery farming, have a very high cholesterol level. Modern feeding and rearing methods for poultry, pigs and cattle have produced the higher cholesterol level in eggs and in the fat of pigs and cows. In the case of the latter, the fat is a much more saturated fat than was formerly the case. Factory farming has depressed real food value by mechanisation and artificial feeding methods.

The key to the problem of cholesterol in the blood lies in the fact that saturated fats are animal fats and dangerous to cholesterol levels and the unsaturated fats are vegetable fats. That is a simplification, for fish oil is an unsaturated fat, but coconut a saturated fat. A more simple basis general rule is that, *at normal room temperatures*, saturated fat is solid, while unsaturated fat is liquid, even in fairly low temperatures.

Cholesterol is important to the system in that it is essential for hormones, which control growth, energy and sexual characteristics and for the insulating sheaths for nerves. It is 'free' cholesterol which, in combination with fat, carries out the above task. But unsaturated fat is the best medium for 'free' cholesterol to blend with.

Caffeine, which is present in coffee, tea, some popular soft drinks and many common drug preparations, is a stimulant. Taken in excess, however, it is over-stimulating, raising the metabolism and, among other things, causing restlessness, nervousness, a raising of cholesterol levels and an excess of uric acid in the system. Uric acid is also present in protein, especially meat. Any excessive consumption of tea and coffee, in conjunction with excesses in animal meat or meat products, leads to an excess of uric acid in the body and increases the prospects of early degenerative diseases, particularly arthritis and arterial diseases.

Toxic Food Additives
Refined carbohydrates and saturated fats constitute a threat to real nutrition. They are made worse because of toxic food additives – pesticides, growth stimulants, preservatives and colouring agents – which contaminate them from the growing stage until they appear on the table. The list of chemicals added to food is endless and it is not until there is concrete proof – usually after tragedies – that any agent is banned. Consider how many years lapsed before D.D.T. came under vigorous control or was banned.

Decreases in resistance to disease and a decline in vitality are too often the harbingers of crippling diseases which, though they may limit life, do not kill. Such crippling diseases, however, especially the various form of arthritis, do not make retired life easy. Unfortunately they can and do make for premature old age.

A reversal of the early degeneration so often encountered is possible, especially when the premature degeneration is very largely the result of incorrect nutrition and not the outcome of accidents, excessive tension or other causes. In all probability nine people out of ten eat their way into an early physical decline.

Inbuilt Resilience

There is an obvious advantage in enjoying correct nutrition from the earliest possible age. On the other hand, fortunately, the human system has a remarkable inbuilt resilience and capacity for compensation and recovery. It is this inherent capacity for healing and resistance to disease which enables life to proceed – admittedly at a less efficient and tolerable level – on a sub-standard diet for years. It is, therefore, possible to reverse or slow up the degeneration. Much will depend upon the age that correct nutrition comes into force.

Natural degeneration is a variable factor. After 50 it may be too late to completely reverse some physical changes. What can be achieved, however, is a reduction in the damage caused by such changes, the arresting of further degeneration and, equally important, a slowing up of the normal and inevitable degeneration associated with age.

The most damaging and negative attitude is to assert that it is too late to change. Even most advanced ages can be helped by correct nutrition. Negative mental attitudes to anything new are often an indication of age. In adult life, a negative and inflexible attitude is frequently an indication of imbalance and a pointer to an early and difficult old age.

With an open mind, and taken at the earliest possible age, the transition from an imbalanced and deficiency diet to correct feeding will ensure health and an easy passage into and through later life. The change-over is neither complicated nor difficult once the fundamentals are grasped. These fundamentals will not be discussed.

Food is arbitrarily divided into protein, carbohydrates, fats, vitamins, mineral salts and water. In its natural state, food provides all the elements required by the body and, as we have already noted, it would be almost impossible to over-indulge in some foods – namely sugar and the common starch foods. There is a further division of food into acid and alkaline elements. The so-called 'protective foods' are those which are rich in vitamins and mineral salts. It is fortunate that, to a large extent, these protective elements are found in the alkaline foods. It is fruit and vegetables which are, in the main, the alkaline and cleansing foods. Another refinement is that some foods tend to create an excess of mucus and cause catarrh. Catarrh is a common ailment. It is also responsible for much of the deafness that afflicts people in older age groups.

Protein
This is found principally in meat, fish, eggs, cheese, nuts and pulse foods. Protein is required for cell growth and repair, but meat particularly is extremely acid-forming. Nitrogen, which is derived from protein, is not stored in the body, but is excreted as urea. Excessive protein in the diet means additional burdens on the liver and an accumulation of uric acid in the body. This, in turn, is one of the major causes of crippling rheumatic disorders. Eggs have a high cholesterol level in addition to protein. Even four eggs per week can be more than adequate. A diet which contains from 10 to 15 per cent protein is more conducive to health than a higher figure, especially for the older person.

Carbohydrates
These are derived from two main sources – starches and sugars. Starch, of course, is principally found in wheat, cereals and potatoes. All sugar (except lactose-milk sugar), comes from beet or cane, with fruit and honey as secondary sources. Carbohydrates are the common *bulk* foods. They contain carbon and supply the body with heat and energy. As such they are essential, but the best sources are those which still contain the essential vitamins and mineral salts. Wholewheat bread, wholegrain cereals, honey, molasses, cane sugar and fruit are the best sources of carbohydrates for the reason that the vitamin and mineral content is largely preserved and they supply a convenient form of roughage necessary for bowel activity.

Fats
Fats are essential for energy and body warmth. Mass production of food via factory farming has left its mark on almost every type of food, to the detriment of its quality. Meat fat, which in any case raises cholesterol levels with possible damage to the cardio-vascular system, is no exception to this rule. The best sources of fat are the essential fatty acids contained in sunflower, corn oil

and other vegetable or fish oils. The latter are the safe fats. Milk and butter also contain fat. Meat fat is contra-indicated and fried foods (even when fried in vegetable oil) should be avoided.

Vitamins and Mineral Salts

These are the protective elements which sustain health and provide the resistance to disease and early degeneration. In normal circumstances, even without a very varied diet, there should be no need for additional vitamins and mineral salts. Synthetic vitamins are a poor substitute for what should be found naturally in food. Natural food provides adequate vitamins and minerals and it is only the refining and adulteration of food that leads to deficiences.

Water

Without water life cannot be sustained, whereas it is quite possible to go for lengthy periods without food and survive. Providing sufficient liquids are taken, in fact, one of the best means of retaining full physical and mental powers to a venerable old age is to fast for three or four days twice a year. No harm will come from fasting if sufficient liquid is taken. On the contrary, such fasting cleanses the system and raises the quality of the blood supply.

Even water is not sacrosanct. Many water supplies are always in danger from pollutants and the addition of fluoride to main water can accelerate hardening of the arteries and rheumatism. Food is roughly from 75 to 90 per cent water and there is no need for literally 'washing out the kidneys' which is so often prescribed. The water contained in fruit and vegetables is the safest water. Many spa waters are now available and are preferable to tap water.

The best guide to rational nutrition is the following:

	Percentage of diet
Protein	10
Carbohydrates	20
Fats	5
Fruit and vegetables	65

For the above to be really effective, however, it is necessary for the carbohydrates to be as natural as possible. This means wholewheat bread and wholegrain cereals (even to brown rice).

The fats should mainly be drawn from vegetable oils and vegetable margarine and the fruit and vegetables organically grown – free from pesticides and chemical fertilizers. The latter is not always feasible despite the steady growth in organic farming.

Cooking Destroys Vitamins

There is another factor which has to be taken into consideration. Cooking inevitably means a loss or destruction of some vitamins and mineral salts. The larger proportion of fruit and vegetables that can be consumed raw provides proportionally additional safeguards. Some raw fruit and at least one raw salad should be part of the daily menu. With advancing age raw food sets a problem of mastication and digestion. This problem and means of overcoming it, will be outlined later.

An excess of acid foods is a characteristic of the average diet. Excessive acidity implies an impure bloodstream and additional work for the organs of elimination – skin, lungs, bowels and kidneys. Acidity is responsible for many minor ailments, ranging from acne to rheumatism. Persistent acidity lays the foundation for chronic diseases in later life.

The following list of acid and alkaline foods is a guide to correct nutrition:

Acid	*Alkaline*
Meat, meat products	Fruit
Fish	Vegetables
Bread, cakes, pastries, pastas	Common herbs
Tea, coffee, cocoa	Edible seaweed
Artificial fruit drinks	
Squashes	
Sweets and chocolate	
Pickles, condiments, jam	

There are exceptions and anomalies in most things. Food is no different. The acid citrus fruits have an alkaline reaction. Experience shows, however, that elderly people suffering from rheumatism or arthritis should avoid oranges. Rhubarb is a very acid fruit which should be avoided. It is high in oxalic acid and deadly to rheumatic victims. Spinach and lettuce, while acceptable to most, should be used sparingly for geriatrics. Tomatoes, plums and prunes can be taken by geriatrics but never extensively.

It will be noted that the alkaline foods, with their high vitamin and mineral content, form the bulk of the diet. It is the alkaline foods, too, which are devoid of mucus-forming elements. Mucus is a very important factor in the etiology of catarrh. An excess of mucus can affect many parts of the body, including the respiratory and digestive tracts and parts of the genito-urinary system. Catarrh is a very prevalent complaint which can be avoided by correct nutrition.

The most notorious mucus-forming foods are listed below in their order of mucosity:

Mucus-forming foods

Chocolate, cocoa
Macaroni, spaghetti and other pastas
Creamy dishes – namely creamy rice pudding
Dairy produce
Cakes and bread (especially those made with white flour and white sugar)
Fried food

Balanced and correct nutrition does not depend on the exclusion of all acid and mucus-forming foods, nor would it be possible to exclude them. Nutrition does, however, depend upon getting such items in their proper proportions. It also depends upon selecting the best of all food divisions, especially where the carbohydrates are involved. A further and not inconsiderable factor is that food must be enjoyed. Too many elderly people come to regard eating purely as a duty.

The maximum protection against disease and early degeneration can only be assured when the maximum advantage is extracted from food. The materials for correct nutrition are there for disposal. To choose not to use them or to violate and denigrate them is a suicidal policy. What is involved in correct nutrition is physical health. Responsibility for health is a personal matter which should not be shirked. Furthermore, few elderly people wish to become a burden to their families or friends. There is no surer way of doing just that, providing life is not suddenly cut short, than by depriving the body of the essential food materials for activity, growth and repair.

CHAPTER FIVE

DIET FOR THE SENIOR CITIZEN

The prevention of degenerative disease is the most significant factor for the senior citizen. Next to prevention comes cure, and then arresting further breakdown. Age cannot be prevented; but its effects can be deferred and effectively minimized. Up to a point most degenerative diseases, once established, are progressive. To halt and arrest that progression is an important victory for the older person.

Each advancing year exacts its toll and adds to past history. Many people do not even learn from experience. The same mistakes are repeated. Correct nutrition is the exception rather than the rule. Apathy, ignorance and prejudice are the enemies of a happy old age. So, too, are frustration, selfishness and excessive tension. Some attitudes are difficult to change, as are some circumstances and environmental conditions. What can be changed, however, is the imbalance in nutrition which is a certain guarantee of early degeneration.

The Most Vulnerable Age

It is claimed that the most apathetic and the most difficult to influence age is the mid-fifties. This is especially so where matters of health are concerned. Yet it is the most vulnerable age and probably one of the most decisive phases of life in relation to later age. It is the age when the reversal of previous poor history in nutrition and other health matters still offers wide scope. To prevent is more important than to cure. And where it is too late for prevention, there is greater possibility of cure or demonstrable arrest of progression.

The less past history of nutritional errors, accidents, tension, over-indulgence, and other indiscretions, the better the prospects are for a longer and more fruitful life. This may seem unimportant in early adult life, but the necessity for care assumes larger proportions with each advancing year. Such care, at the same time, should be kept in balance and not develop into a morbid routine for self-preservation. This in itself would be self-defeating and probably induce nervous diseases. *To think and act positively and still enjoy life is a surer way to health.*

The popular theory that after a certain age it is too late to change is a fallacy. *It is never too late*. Even in advanced years, despite the slowing down of metabolism, the body retains a great deal of resilience and recuperative powers. These can be impaired by the negative attitude adopted by many older people. With a positive attitude and a sound mental approach, however, it is possible to create a much improved level of health, even in the elderly. Providing that the cells of the body are receiving correct nutrition and blood supply is not suffering from gross interference, then there is very little difference in the healing capacity of the old or the young.

While the basis for correct nutrition remains as previously outlined, there is an obvious necessity for adaptation to advancing years. With reduced physical activity less food is required. But the reduction in food should mainly be in the carbohydrates, not the proteins or vegetables and fruit. With decreased physical activity calorie requirements are reduced.

Basic Calorie Requirements

In the very old, especially old people living alone, there is a tendency not to bother about food and to produce an artifically low appetite. Boredom sometimes creates the reverse condition. This state, however, is more likely to apply in the early days of retirement and more so with males. It has been estimated that the basic calorie requirement for men of 60 and over is 1,500 a day and for women 1,250, though these are subject to variations according to activity.

The danger of over-eating, especially in early retirement years, is always present. This creates a tendency to obesity with added dangers of limiting already reduced physical movement. Active movement is as vital to the elderly as to the young. Movement is essential to the circulation and freedom of joints. Elderly people can easily succumb to resting too frequently and for too long periods when in actual fact they would be physically better equipped if they exerted more effort in movement. It is a disservice to encourage older people to eat more and take long periods of rest.

It is in this respect that power tools, which reduce so much of the physical effort in house-work, gardening and hobbies, must be used with discretion. The younger person – especially those between the ages of 30 to 55 – too frequently succumbs to the temptations of reducing physical effort to a minimum. The pressure of time is often advanced as the reason for purchasing power aids. It is a very good reason, but care must be taken that sufficient physical effort is used in one direction or another.

Decreased Food Consumption

While the normal three meals per day are quite in order when full physical powers are retained, as physical activity lessens, so the quantity of food consumed should be decreased. Not just that, however, but the character and frequency of meals require some alteration. No fixed age can be set for changes in meals – so much depends upon the individual. Good previous health history, beneficial hereditary influences and freedom from undue stress, all contribute. As a general rule, however, a gradual adaptation should commence between 65 and 70.

Age produces an inevitable decline in the powers of digestion, absorption and assimilation and these have to be taken into account. With the reduction in true appetite also becoming more pronounced with the advancing years, additional safeguards have to be taken to counteract any possible deficiencies. For the elderly person living alone there is a tendency to neglect meals or even to exist on titbits. Forgetfulness, too, is a real danger. Pride, or the danger of being thought incapable, will frequently make the really old person assert that his or her meals are regular and adequate when quite the reverse is the case.

Memory Difficulties

Ageing can produce difficulties with memory. Premature ageing and loss of memory is a little-understood phenomenon. A research programme at the London Institute of Neurology under Professor Alan Davison is probing this very problem. One of the lines of research involved is investigating the cause of fatty deposits in the cells of prematurely aged adults. In premature ageing, the brain cells die at a faster rate. Unfortunately they cannot regenerate, as other body cells do.

Memory is an important faculty. Correct nutrition has an obvious connection in preserving the memory. Excessive fat consumption, among other things, is implicated in the degeneration of physical and mental powers. It is more than probable that both Vitamin B12 and Vitamin E would stave off the decline in mental powers and memory.

All life is a process of change. With the gradual decline in physical powers there is a decline in blood circulation and reduced compensation and accommodation to thermal and other changes. Absorption and assimilation of nutriment is also reduced. Effective nutrition depends upon a good and clean blood supply. Reduced food consumption, absorption and assimilation, therefore, demands that the quality of the food should be of the highest order. In age, for instance, calcium absorption is frequently impaired and this, with possible Vitamin D deficiency leads to osteoporosis and fragile bones. Broken bones are the nightmare of the very senior person.

Because absorption and assimilation is imperfect in age, nutritional hazards such as calcium deficiency and reduced haemoglobin content of the blood, leading to fragile bones and anaemia, can easily arise. All the vitamins and mineral salts required in early days are just as essential to the elderly. It has been suggested by some authorities that a deficiency of Vitamin B12 can be associated with decline in mental powers and with mental abnormalities. Vitamin E for instance, has an effect on the stability of essential fatty acids, and the diet must contain both vitamins and acids if it is to be effective. The truth is that the system cannot afford any vitamin or mineral deficiency, since interaction is always taking place. Where there is a decline in absorption and assimilation, vitamin and mineral supplements are often necessary in our sophisticated society. They can be even more essential to the senior citizen, whose absorption and assimilation are normally less efficient and deficiencies more easily arise. The over-riding factor in nutrition for older people, therefore, is the need for less bulk, reduction in carbohydrates and the maintenance of an effective supply of protective elements in an easily digested and assimilated form, even if some of the latter are in supplement form.

Liquidizing Raw Foods

Raw salads provide vitamins, mineral salts and bulk, but present problems of digestion to elders. This problem, however, is easily overcome by placing the same salad ingredients into a liquidizer and reducing them into a semi-liquid and digestible form. The same problem, though not acute, arises with some cooked vegetables. A liquidizer again solves the problems. Raw fruit, such as apples and pears, can undergo similar treatment.

It is possible to digest and assimilate a great deal of raw food when it is liquidized. Some vitamin loss may be caused, but less than from cooking. It is one of the best means of ensuring that nutritional balance is being maintained. A further manner in which it is possible to conveniently absorb nutriment is by taking natural fruit and vegetable juices.

The one possible danger with liquidized raw food – but this applies to many other foods as well – is that it will be gulped down. Time must be taken in eating the food and it must be masticated thoroughly to ensure digestion, assimilation and absorption. Ultimately it is only the nutriment that is assimilated and absorbed that sustains life.

Ageing is a continuous and gradual process. There can be a lengthy transition period, therefore, from normal methods of feeding to that of an older age level. What should take place, of course, is that, as physical activity decreases, so should the natural appetite. Smaller meals, with a little snack in between, are better than three main meals. The nutrition plan outlined for very senior people should only begin when there is an obvious need. What is recommended, however, is that it should be commenced immediately by those elderly people who have previously existed on an imbalanced diet. Younger people – and they can never be too young – should base their diet on the nutritional advice previously outlined. The more years of sound nutrition that are possessed, the more freedom there will be from degenerative diseases.

A Lacto-vegetarian Diet

The protein in the balanced diet mentioned, and in that outlined below, need not be largely that of animal products. Meat and meat products have many disadvantages, one of which is the high putrefaction rate of such products. This is an important factor when a possible intestinal stasis has to be taken into account. Vegetarians or near-vegetarians can easily supply their 10% protein from diary produce, the pulse foods, nuts and soya beans and flour made from that source. It must also be remembered that a certain amount of protein is present in cereals, including bread, and no protein deficiency need arise when vegetarianism is practised.

Cutting down animal protein reduces the uric acid level in the bloodstream. Vegetarians usually display either an alkaline urine or one with considerably less acid than that found in meat eaters. This is a distinct advantage and one of some influence on degenerative diseases, especially those of the musculo-skeletal system and the liver. Gout, for instance, is associated with an excess of meat products in the diet.

With meat and fish there also exists the danger that the protein requirements can be too easily exceeded. Meat eaters rarely forego that additional protein found in other foods such as eggs, cheese and the many convenience foods now available.

The possible disadvantage of a lacto-vegetarian diet in the older person is that, in reducing the total food intake, the reduction may lead to a deficiency of protein and amino-acids in the body. The danger, though small, does exist. Such a risk, however, could be countered by additional care or by the inclusion of a little fish in the diet. A further factor is that not more than four eggs per week should be eaten because of their high cholesterol content. The four eggs per week are distinct from those indirectly used in food. Cholesterol levels are best maintained at safe levels when meat and meat products are excluded from the diet.

There is no doubt that, on the whole, a lacto-vegetarian regime has definite advantages. This has been proven time after time, especially when health and longevity has been investigated. The lessons of two World Wars have corroborated this fact. During these wars, when meat and sugar were rationed and the necessity to conserve grain and other cereals produced the darker (and coarser) but more nutritious loaf, the level of public health in the countries affected displayed remarkable improvement while the stringencies lasted.

Diet Plan for the Senior Citizen

First thing	Weak cup of tea or diluted fruit juice Honey for sweetening, if desired
Breakfast	Muesli Glass skimmed milk or 2 slices wholemeal toast, butter and honey Prunes or grated raw apple Glass of skimmed milk
Mid-morning	Yeast extract with skimmed milk or coffee (preferably dandelion coffee) or fruit juice with two digestive biscuits
Lunch	Steamed fish with potato Any green or root vegetable Baked or stewed apple or Cauliflower or leek or onion *au gratin* Carrots or other root vegetables

2 baked or mashed bananas
or
Lamb with grilled tomato
Potato and root vegetable in season
Soaked dates or melon or soft fruit
or
Baked potato with cheese
Green and root vegetable
Baked or stewed apple or pear
or
Nut savoury or egg dish
Green or root vegetable
Stewed apricots or prunes
or
Meat and vegetable stew with whole barley
Potato
Pineapple or melon or mashed banana
or
Poached or scrambled egg with tomato
Green and root vegetable
Baked or stewed apple
or
Cheese, tomato and onion savoury
Baked or steamed potato with a green vegetable
Baked or mashed banana
or
Cold meat with potatoes
Tomato salad or cauliflower or green vegetable
Melon or pineapple or grated raw apple

Tea

Weak tea with 2 digestive biscuits or
yeast extract sandwiches

Supper

Liquidized salad
Biscuits or 2 thin slices brown bread and butter
Cottage cheese or baked potato or
mushroom or egg
or
Thick vegetable soup
Toast or biscuits and butter
Fresh fruit
or
Baked potato and grilled tomatoes
Cottage cheese
Fresh or dried fruit

Last thing

Cup of slippery elm food
made with skimmed milk.

Note Sunflower oil and cider vinegar should be added to the salads. Herbs
should be used freely, especially parsley and chives. Garlic in some
form or other – natural garlic or garlic oil capsules – should be taken

daily. Garlic is a good internal antiseptic and useful in all chest complaints. Recommended raw juices are apple, grape or orange juice in the fruit category and carrot and beetroot in the vegetable category. An excellent combination is apple, beetroot, carrot and a little celery. Being home produced it can be made in sufficient quantity to last two days if kept in a refrigerator. *Raw vegetable or fruit juices must be sipped slowly.*

Meals can be even further simplified and there is nothing wrong with monotony, providing the essential ingredients are in the diet. A simple meal of wholemeal bread and butter or vegetable margarine, cottage cheese, raw onion and an apple is quite in order. Again, thick vegetable soup with a little non-fat meat, 2 slices of wholemeal bread and butter or vegetable margarine and a few prunes or soaked dates can suffice. Even a poached egg on toast with raw or grilled tomatoes and a grated raw apple is also sufficient. It must be remembered, however, that the carbohydrates must be kept down, fat and sugars limited, condiments very much reduced and not more than four eggs per week should be eaten.

Liquid with meals should be avoided, and despite the fact that balanced nutrition provides more liquid than orthodox meals, extra fluid may still be required. Drinking *between* meals is advised, as and when necessary. Previous mention has been made of the fact that providing sufficient liquid has been taken, life can be sustained without food for many days. Older people are not generally advised to fast, but one day on liquids alone now and again can be beneficial, providing that sufficient liquid is consumed during that day.

Balanced nutrition is, apart from severe accidents, the most important single factor in the pursuit of health, long life and freedom from the worst effects of degenerative diseases. Even those who have not had the benefit of sound hereditary and environmental influences can benefit from the effects of balanced nutrition.

Some diseases inevitably limit life. Where life is not cut short, however, there is a huge need to improve physical standards to the pitch where freedom of movement, mental powers and capacity to enjoy life can be maintained. This is a moral duty which, with the vast growth in numbers of senior citizens, requires urgent attention. Furthermore, since it is the individual's own future health and happiness that is at risk, it is a personal responsibility to maintain the highest possible standard of health at all ages.

A Controversial Nutritionist

Adelle Davis, a successful but controversial American nutritionist, wrote her first book on diet and healthy eating in 1946. Her recommended diet is mainly the same as the one I endorse, but with more emphasis on vitamin and mineral supplements. She also condemns the average deficiency diet based on refined and denatured foods.

In an interview published in the *Daily Telegraph Supplement* of November 1973, Adelle Davis said, speaking of her early days as a nutritionist:

> Nutrition was in a very early stage then, you understand. There were no vitamin supplements apart from cod liver oil. Not a great deal of research had been done and doctors were very ignorant as to how nutrition could build health. I became more and more convinced that what was necessary – and possible – was to forestall illness by supplying the body with the right fuels. All the time I was gaining practical experience with patients. I would discover that certain foods contributed certain things.

The books Adelle Davis has written are aimed at using diet for the prevention of disease, and it is this field that is so important to people of all ages, but particularly in the middle and later years when preventative action is still possible.

Professor George Briggs of the University of California at Berkeley, is a nutritionist and states that: 'More than a third of all chronic illnesses in America, which account for 83 % of adult male deaths are diet-related.'

One American authority on nutrition who disagrees with the claims of Adelle Davis did however mention two important facts about the American habits of eating: 'They'd be better fed if they ate less and exercised more.'

The weight of evidence for maintaining health, preventing disease and delaying the degenerative effects of life, is that a balanced diet of organically-grown food (or food as little contaminated or denatured as possible), is absolutely vital. With the passing of years, less food need be consumed and physical activity should be maintained. But the food consumed must provide the essential ingredients for health and the earlier the process of correct nutrition commences, the greater the possibilities of extending a useful and active life.

CHAPTER SIX

VASCULAR AND CARDIO-VASCULAR DISEASES

As age progresses the arteries suffer a slight decrease in muscle tissue, which is replaced by fibrous tissue. The hardening, thickening and loss of elasticity in the blood-vessels is loosely termed arterio-sclerosis and it is one of the degenerative diseases in geriatrics. That arteries thicken and become more tortuous is of less importance than the state of the lumen (space) in the vessel. When this is narrowed by degeneration the blood-pressure must rise in compensation. Hypertension and arterio-sclerosis, therefore, are common findings as age increases.

The hypertension from normal degenerative changes in the arteries is termed essential hypertension and a raised systolic pressure can be quite consistent with health. The degeneration by calcification and reduction in elasticity increases the pressure required to propel the blood through the arteries. Under normal circumstances, and in good health, the degeneration is a slow process. The rise in blood-pressure, therefore, is not dramatic. Hypertension is not necessarily a sequela of ageing, despite this state being a relatively common finding.

Hardening of the arteries is a normal degenerative process. Like all degenerative diseases its onset, extent and severity depend upon past history. Under ordinary circumstances, however, such degeneration is a slow process. A low blood-pressure can persist throughout life and be compatible with health. Where, over the years, the blood-pressure has steadily remained below the average, this can be a positive advantage in latter years. Vegetarians and lacto-vegetarians, people who have avoided animal fats or have led abstemious lives, tend to have a lower than average blood-pressure.

Persistent Stress
Stress and tension are part and parcel of life. Blood-pressure will always rise in moments of stress or excessive emotion – especially anger or fear. Normal stresses and tensions present few problems. Under duress the blood-pressure will temporarily rise and then revert to normal. Persistent stress, however, by creating a history of over-stimulation, inevitably leads to a permanent

hypertension. This is not simply by virtue of the stress, but because such stress is usually accompanied by an excessive intake of either stimulating food or drink (meat, sugar, alcohol, tea, coffee), or nicotine from smoking.

Blood-pressure is dependent upon the heart's capacity to propel the blood, the elasticity and amount of space in the arteries, and the peripheral resistance, namely the resistance of the finer arterial network. In age it can be accepted that there will be an increase of systolic blood-pressure, in other words, the pressure coinciding with the contraction of the heart, but there need not necessarily be an increase in the diastolic or resting phase. The increase in the systolic pressure is, of course, dependent upon previous history and, in fact, little or no change in blood-pressure can even be experienced in a healthy old person, but such people are usually slim and have had a sparse, perhaps monotonous diet, and have practised moderation.

There is a normal increase in blood-pressure from childhood to middle and later ages. The increase, however, is a very variable factor, depending to a large extent on previous history, temperament, nutrition and weight. A slim, placid person with a history of moderate habits will tend to keep his or her blood-pressure on the lower and safer side. A blood-pressure reading for an older person would be considered good if it stood at or about 160 systolic and 90 diastolic. But many active elderly people have systolic pressures varying between 110 and 210 and diastolic pressures between 60 and 110. There can, therefore, be a fairly wide range of figures for blood-pressure in age without any disastrous physical handicap.

Blood-pressure suffers the same variations in age as in younger life. It will rise with excitement, tension, stress, and anger, as it will if there is a combination of heat and undue activity. The danger from hypertension in the elderly, therefore, is that if the usual blood-pressure is high, and it is subject to further strain, then the conditions for a stroke are present.

Reduction of Activity and Tension
One of the advantages of age is that ambition and the competitive urge decline, physical activity is reduced and tension, on the whole, is reduced. These factors combine to keep life on a lower key and reduce the necessity for the frequent upsurges in bloodpressure which are so common in normal competitive existence. Tensions and anxieties are common

amongst older people, though usually not on the same scale as in earlier days. All tensions, however, tend to raise blood-pressure. On the other hand, obesity and incorrect feeding usually present the larger problem when hypertension is a danger.

Arterio-sclerosis and hypertension are all too common in age. Cerebral haemorrhage from a rupture of one of the smaller arteries in the brain, or cerebral embolism from interruption to the blood supply by a blood clot, or bacterial matter, are the common result of degeneration in the arteries.

Prolonged hypertension causes exhaustion, dyspnoea and enlargement of the heart. Where obesity is an added complication or even an indirect cause, there is a much greater risk to life. But the risk is not just to life: there is also the danger of complete or partial paralysis, which is often feared more than death.

Arterio-sclerosis is such a frequent symptom in old age that it is accepted as inevitable. To a certain extent this is the case. But it is the degree of arterio-sclerosis which is important. Atheroma (patchy degeneration in the walls of the large arteries) is caused by arterio-sclerosis. Degenerative changes such as arterio-sclerosis and atheroma cause thrombosis (formation of a blood clot), embolism (obstruction or shutting up of a small blood-vessel by a transported clot, vegetation, or small mass of bacteria), and aneurysm (dilation of an artery due to the vessel wall yielding and being subjected to stretching by the pressure of the blood).

These changes affect the larger arteries more than the smaller. Obstruction to blood flow, however, especially in the lower limbs, is often due to degenerative changes. Atheroma is frequently situated behind the knee joint, where previous strain or injury is quite common. Interference to the blood supply in the legs and feet can be severe and much depends upon the alternative 'collateral' blood-vessels taking up and compensating for the obstruction.

Principal Causes of Strokes

Arterial degeneration and hypertension are the principal causes of strokes, whether the stroke is due to cerebral thrombosis or cerebral embolism or the rupture of a small artery in the brain. In advanced age or prolonged years of hypertension there can be transient and small disturbances of consciousness or short attacks of mental confusion. Such attacks often follow a period of more than usual physical or mental activity. The danger of this type of attack is a serious fall with its possibilities of fractured bones.

The normal treatment for hypertension is to administer anti-hypertensive drugs, impose some restriction in diet to reduce weight, and advise the sufferer to cut down on salt. But anti-hypertension drugs are not without their dangers, especially of depression. Preventing or delaying arterial degeneration is much more important. Nature's own anti-hypertensive properties are contained in a good balanced diet, especially when it includes such items as edible seaweed and buckwheat. Food supplements such as seaweed tablets or rutin (the latter in tea or tablet form) are also useful. That blood-pressure can rise gradually over the years, with little or no real damage to health, is a positive indication that correct nutrition, mobility, moderate habits and good posture can preserve youth and limit the disadvantages of age. Age, too, does not limit healing capacity. Even many years of neglect and abuse can be remedied by attention to diet: the cleaning of the bloodstream by increasing the efficiency of the lungs, skin, bowels and kidneys; the reduction of surplus weight and by ensuring spinal integrity and a good posture.

Hypertension in the not-so-old is often indicated when there is a throbbing headache combined with vertigo, head noises and occasional vomiting. Where, however, in the older person, the persistent rise to the higher levels of blood-pressure has been a gradual process, these signs are frequently absent. Many old people can have hypertension without being fully aware of it, because the accommodation to the change has been going on over the years.

Arterial Embolism
The weakness, exhaustion and breathlessness of hypertension and degenerative changes in the arterial system is aggravated when the person is obese or when the heart or lungs are involved. Arterial embolism can arise when clots escape from vegetations on heart valves. Emboli often lodge at the position where an artery branches off and its lumen is narrowed. Embolism is not confined to the cerebral arteries. It can also develop in the limbs, where occlusion of one of the smaller arteries can cause serious circulatory problems.

Blood is pumped from the heart into the large aorta artery. From the aorta, other arteries branch off, carrying the blood to all parts of the body. The heart itself, however, requires a blood supply, and this comes from the two coronary arteries which branch off from the base of the aorta and supply the heart muscle by still smaller branches. It is the coronary arteries which, when blocked, cause the coronary thrombosis and cut off the supply of blood to the heart itself.

Atherosclerosis is a term which is gradually supplanting the more generalized arterio-sclerosis. Atheroma is the term for patchy degeneration, as we have seen. Degeneration in the coronary arteries can go undetected and, since their space is small, it takes very little to completely block a coronary artery, which, over the years, has had its space gradually narrowed by other sclerotic changes. Previous mention has been made of the dangers of a diet which contains too much white flour, white sugar, salt and animal fat. The latter, in particular, is strongly implicated in the etiology of coronary disease.

Women Suffer Less

In the younger 40-50 age group, women suffer less from coronary disease and hypertension than men. In later years, however, the incidence of coronary thrombosis tends to equalize, especially in the seventies. One of the reasons advanced for this is that women, in their earlier years, have a lower cholesterol level than men. This lower cholesterol level is associated with the female sex hormone and it is only after the menopause that the cholesterol level substantially increases. Women, therefore, up to the menopause have some inbuilt protection against high cholesterol levels which men lack.

The fact that women have a higher tolerance to fat during their younger years does not imply that they should eat more animal fats than men. Animal fat is acid-forming and causes digestive troubles, quite apart from its high cholesterol level. The unsaturated fats − sunflower, corn and fish oil, and others − are the safe fats which help to avoid atherosclerosis and coronary thrombosis. Women should not delude themselves into thinking that a coronary or gastric ulcer is primarily a male disease.

Powers of Compensation

Nature makes many attempts to compensate or meet special demands. Rises in temperature, pulse, blood-pressure, are all normal reactions to specific and temporary requirements. The heart has remarkable powers of compensation and can adapt to new situations which throw more demands upon it. Adjustments are also made on a permanent basis, namely the gradual increase in blood-pressure in age to counter arterial degeneration. Enlargement of the heart is a common enough condition in the elderly, where valvular disease of the heart, hypertension or anaemia have existed for some time. Moderate and gradual enlargement of the heart can be well tolerated in the elderly, providing other complications are minimized.

Anaemia, diabetes and obesity – all largely nutritional disorders – contribute to ischaemic heart disease, which is a sequela of coronary artery disorder because of interference with the supply of blood to the heart.

Degeneration of the heart in the elderly is the result of fatty degeneration, the growth of fibrous tissue between the muscle fibres and the wasting of the heart muscles. The common form of vulvular disease is endocarditis, which is of rheumatic origin and causes small nodules to form on the heart valves.

The heart is a muscular pump which can, to some degree, adapt itself to the demands made upon it. To fulfil its purpose, however, it is dependent upon an unrestricted and clean blood supply. Apart from congenital defects, the condition of the heart valves, muscles and tissues in the elderly is a question of previous general health, nutrition and moderation. Chronic valvular disease is a fairly rife complaint amongst the elderly, with rheumatism, atherosclerotic changes and fatty degeneration as the major causes.

Normal degeneration at later ages must be anticipated, but degeneration is delayed or accelerated according to previous history. Freedom from diseases which affect the heart is a valuable factor in age. But the conditions for preventing heart trouble are the same conditions which prevent most diseases, whether acute, chronic or degenerative. The unity of the body is an inescapable fact.

Resistance to disease and the curtailment of all degenerative disorders – the heart included – lie in correct nutrition, normal functioning of the eliminative processes, a free blood flow, mobility, good posture and the avoidance of excessive stress. Freedom from accidents and a good environment are an added bonus. Providing the first conditions apply, however, nature's ability to compensate and adapt is an invaluable asset. Occasional abuses can be allowed – persistent abuse shortens life.

Other Circulatory Problems

Hypertension and heart conditions are a familiar picture. But other circulatory problems are part of normal existence. Varicositis and varicose ulcers are often dreaded by older people, especially those who have had a history of varicose veins. Women who have borne several children are often more prone to varicose veins. Improved methods of childbirth and after-care, however, are reducing these effects.

Varicose veins have become dilated and stretched out of proportion to the quantity of blood they transport. For mechanical reasons, it is usually the lower part of the body which is affected, since the venous blood has to be propelled back to the heart. Piles (haemorrhoids), and varicocele (or varicose condition of the testicles) and the veins of the thighs and legs are the common sites.

Weakness in the walls of the veins is sometimes hereditary, but it is usually caused by stagnation of the blood-flow from sedentary occupations, standing too long and from too-tight garments which restrict the blood-flow. Exercise provides the pumping action that muscular contraction exerts in emptying the veins. The stagnant blood dilates and weakens the walls of the veins, and the valves – provided to assist the upward flow of the blood – become useless.

Risk of Varicose Ulcer

With increasing stagnation and weakness, the condition spreads to other veins. The importance of strengthening the veins and restoring venous circulation is obvious. In the elderly and slow-moving person there is always a risk of a varicose ulcer if the condition is neglected. This arises when the poorly nourished skin around the veins becomes eczematous and irritable and is scratched. Such an ulcer is difficult to heal when blood circulation is poor and congestion is present.

The treatment of varicose veins by surgery or injection is not always satisfactory and does not remove the cause. When a varicose condition does arise one of the most efficient antidotes is to subject the limbs to frequent spraying with cold water. Cold water reduces the inflammation and stimulates the flow of blood. Despite the fact that massage is normally contra-indicated in varicose veins, careful massage can and will improve the circulation in the limbs. Even varicose ulcers can eventually heal when finger massage applied around the ulcer restores circulation and improves the nutrition of the damaged area.

Symptoms of Vein Inflammation

Inflammation of a vein is a serious matter, principally because of the clotting of the blood that usually takes place within the inflamed part. There is always a risk that a clot may break up and portions of it be transported by the blood to lodge in other vessels. Phlebitis (thrombo-phlebitis) is the common name for such a condition, which is usually caused by an injury, bruise or fracture, especially when there is restriction to blood-flow, as in varicose veins. The symptoms of such inflammation are swelling around and below the part affected, heat, tenderness. When a clot forms in the vein, the vein can be felt as a hard line.

Inordinate and prolonged standing, like prolonged rest, is damaging to blood circulation. Movement is vital to the blood and to the nourishment of cells. Where, however, because of age or physical limitations, movement is curtailed, the legs should be raised when resting – either supported on a stool if sitting or, better still, lying back with the legs completely raised.

While hereditary influences predispose to varicosities, and occupational hazards are present, there is much that can be done to prevent varicose veins. Correct nutrition, attention to oxygen demands and the mobility of limbs and blood-flow are prerequisites of avoiding varicose veins. Haemorrhoids, for instance, would hardly exist if the normal diet was balanced and contained sufficient natural roughage to ensure correct bowel function.

Chronic Constipation

Where constipation has been habitually treated by purgatives and has established itself as a chronic condition, the tendency to haemorrhoids is greater. Stagnation of the bowels, followed by over-stimulation with purgatives, leads to further bowel inactivity. Over-stimulation causes depression. This is a natural law. Many people actually cause constipation by being over-anxious about bowel movements. With decreased activity, older people are inclined to constipation and haemorrhoids. Three factors are usually involved: unbalanced diet, a readiness to take purgatives and a tendency to strain at stool. Diet should be amended along the lines already shown and the latter avoided.

Varicocele is improved when the venous blood-flow is increased. Constipation is a frequent background to varicocele.

Stagnation, pressure effects from the bowels and a lack of abdominal movement contribute to varicocele. Deep-breathing provides oxygen and removes CO_2 from the blood. Diaphragmatic breathing involves the abdominal muscles – on expiration the abdominal muscles contract and sink down – on inspiration the abdominal muscles rise. If this exercise is carried out on the floor, with the knees slightly raised, the varicocele will diminish.

Older people bruise easily. A great deal of this is due to fragile capillaries. This condition is partly due to restriction to blood-flow and partly to vitamin deficiency, especially vitamins K and P. Both of these are present in a normal balanced diet. Vitamin K is found in leafy vegetables, tomatoes and liver and Vitamin P in citrus fruits. Correct nutrition should supply all requirements, but vitamin supplements are sometimes necessary.

Prevention, it must be emphasized, is better than cure. Preventative methods can avoid much pain and misery. Where a condition has commenced, however, steps to eradicate it should be adopted. In this connection not only is diet important, but simple hydropathic measures can supplement diet and other therapies. Hydrotherapy will be discussed in Chapter Twelve.

CHAPTER SEVEN

RHEUMATISM AND ARTHRITIS

Rheumatism and arthritis are crippling complaints which frequently appear in very early middle age. This breeds the idea that such diseases are inevitable in later life. Neglected rheumatism, or rheumatism which is solely treated by toxic pain-killing drugs, is almost bound to become an arthritic condition in the end.

Many factors are involved in the cause of both rheumatism and arthritis. In arthritis, especially gouty arthritis, there is usually a history of excessive proteins and uric acid (meat, meat products, heavy wines and other purines), while those suffering from rheumatoid arthritis often have a low tolerance for carbohydrates. The real degenerative form of arthritis, however, is osteoarthritis, for which normal wear and tear and breakdown of cartilage is a feature. In most elderly people with arthritis there exists a combination of rheumatism, osteo and rheumatoid arthritis.

Any limitation of movement, whether it is caused by actual limitation, or fear of moving the joint because of pain, reduces the circulation and nourishment around that area. The longer this process continues, the greater the damage. In youth and early adult life there is a natural tendency to move the restricted joint as early as possible. In later ages, however, there is often a tendency to over-protect and avoid pain, thus increasing the possibility of degeneration in the joint. Age, too, has to contend with previous injuries which, though nature may have made compensation, have left some scarring.

Previous history plays a tremendous part in the degenerative diseases. Environment, occupation, nutrition, posture, accidents, stress, abuse, misuse and hereditary influences are variable factors, but each contribute.

A Commonplace Disease
Rheumatism is a commonplace disease, all too often dismissed as an inevitable affliction for which little can be done. Normally it is suppressed by pain-killing drugs (aspirin is a common example), which, while providing relief, do not attack the cause. In most cases it is caused by the excessive consumption of acid-

forming foods, including an excessive intake of proteins, animal fats and refined carbohydrates. Purines (nucleo-proteins which, in metabolism, produce an excess of uric acid), feature in the cause of rheumatism and arthritis. To the excessive acidity of the diet must be added the effects of exposure, over-use or mis-use of the joints and connective tissues, stress and over-stimulation.

The suppression of acute disease is one of the biggest factors in causing chronic ailments. Suppression ignores the cause and, in the case of rheumatism, where aspirin-type drugs are the common treatment, the pain may be relieved temporarily. Such respite, however, is only at the cost of increased acidity, indigestion, a toxic bloodstream and even the possibility of internal haemorrhage.

Unless attempts are made to redress the imbalance in diet by reducing proteins and carbohydrates and increasing the alkaline elements, no progress will be made in the treatment of rheumatism or other afflictions of the musculoskeletal system. Even when the diet is corrected, other abuses such as excessive alcohol, smoking, fatigue and exposure, must be avoided. Changes in weather, damp, and cold draughts, cannot entirely be avoided. Nor is it wise to be over-protective.

The real protection against rheumatism lies in correct nutrition, the avoidance of excesses (stress, fatigue, alcohol), mobility, and in building up the circulation and tone of the skin. The latter is important in that it supplies greater protection to draughts and changes in atmosphere. Hot baths may be temporarily comforting. Heat draws blood from the interior of the body to the superficial areas. This action does not increase circulation and, in time, has a debilitating effect. Extreme heat, like extreme cold, should be avoided by elderly people. Young and active people, however, can improve circulation by having a hot bath (or sauna), providing it is terminated by a cold shower. Heat draws the blood to the surface, the cold drives it back into the deeper vessels. Since, however, the blood must return to the superficial areas, the circulation is increased and stabilized. The 'pull and push' effect of heat and cold increases the general circulation and tones the skin, giving it greater protection against draughts. The skin is also a vital organ of elimination and, when its efficiency is increased, waste products are excreted more freely. The best protection against rheumatism is correct nutrition, an unrestricted blood-flow, mobility, and an efficient skin regulator.

Sacral Tilt

Previous history is the determining factor in age. A long history of rheumatism is usually present in chronic arthritis. Localized arthritis, however, is frequently the result of previous trauma or overuse. Injuries to the knees in more active days leave scar tissue which, by gradual degeneration, is converted into arthritis. Arthritis of the hips and knees can be the result of earlier attacks of so-called 'lumbago' where the principal symptom has been low back pain, but where, in fact, there has been unsuspected malposition of the lumbo-sacral or sacral area. This malposition has created a shift in the weight-bearing, placing a stress upon the hips and the lower spine. A sacral tilt, in fact, making one leg shorter than the other, is quite common. In an effort to maintain the vertical position, sacral tilts involve a gradual curvature of the lumbar area with a corresponding compensation by a curve in the upper thoracic and cervical region.

Where there has been a history of bad posture, accidents, or vertebral lesions, degeneration in the musculoskeletal system is a question of time. Gross interference with mobility and nutrition in and around a joint will, over a period, cause arthritis of one form or another, ankylosis (abnormal immobility and consolidation of the bones of a joint), spondylitis (inflammation of cartilage in the spinal joints) and osteoporosis (reduction in bone mass leaving the bone brittle), and so on. Osteoporosis, though partly a deficiency disease caused by prolonged calcium loss or calcium deficiency, is still influenced by the twin factors of congestion and interference with nutrition by poor or obstructed circulation.

The upright position, with weight-bearing stresses imposed upon the lower lumbar verterbrae, the sacrum and the hips, gives frequent rise to pain in normal life. 'Low back' pain is a familiar symptom. Obesity, bad posture and long periods of standing aggravate this condition. Degeneration, therefore, usually occurs first in the lumbo-sacral area, though the knees are quite often involved at the same time.

Osteo-arthritis

This is the common degenerative form of arthritis. A great deal is due to normal wear and tear, but aggravated by previous history. It is normally progressive. Obesity, which places added strains upon the musculoskeletal system and limits mobility, is a contributory factor. In osteo-arthritis the first change is a breakdown of articular cartilage. Over-growth of bone from calcification and osteophyte formation eventually takes place and this causes eburnation (bone degeneration), and limitation of movement. Arthritis nodules on the fingers are common in age and, in fact, can be present when there is little or no arthritis in other parts of the body.

Degenerative arthritis normally attacks the weight-bearing structures first, either because of obesity, normal stress or a sedentary occupation, limiting movement and circulation. The cervical spine and shoulders, however, are frequently involved. Posture and tension undoubtedly play a part here, since they interfere with nutrition and circulation and cause muscle contraction. Even the jaw bones can be affected by degenerative arthritis, a progressive but often painless disorder.

Where muscle spasm has been present there is a protective or even conscious rigidity and consequent limitation of movement. The limited movement becomes even more limited by the avoidance of activity. Every effort has to be made to retain movement and avoid contractures. While fatigue must be avoided, sufficient movement should be made to prevent the joints from becoming fixed. This is especially the case with the knees. One of the best and simplest exercises is to sit on a table or high chair and 'swing' the legs. This allows the knees to bend more freely.

Rheumatoid Arthritis

Linked with swelling and an overgrowth of connective tissue. The synovial tissues and membrane are involved. The enlargement and swelling is accompanied by muscular wasting. The wrists and hands are usually the most affected parts, but any joint may be affected, particularly the knees and elbows.

In the acute stage of rheumatoid arthritis there is a great deal of muscle spasm and pain. The tendency, therefore, is to maintain the joint in a fixed and more comfortable position. There is also a great deal of local inflammation, with heat and swelling a feature, in both the acute and sub-acute stage. At this juncture, manipulation, which can be a very valuable therapy in arthritis, is contra-indicated. Hydrotherapeutic measures, however, such as cold packs and tepid baths, are beneficial and provide much relief.

In rheumatoid arthritis the joint surfaces are attacked, the cartilage breaks up and the adjacent bone becomes rarefied. Fibrous tissue is laid down around and within the joint and fibrous or bony consolidation may permanently stiffen the joint. Sometimes, when movement is still possible, a loud creaking noise may be made when the joint is moved.

Deformities in rheumatoid arthritis are often the result of prolonged resting of the painful joint, and of secondary contractures of adjacent muscles. Early and suitable exercises when the acute symptoms have subsided can achieve a partial cure, relief, and certainly mitigate the effects of the ailment. Such relief depends upon how promptly corrective measures are applied and the previous health history. Even in advanced age, providing the general state is good, there is much that can be achieved.

Osteo-arthritis is a slower, degenerative type of arthritis, in which the degeneration is governed by previous history, accidents and an imbalance (especially of proteins), in the diet. In rheumatoid arthritis, much the same history is involved, but with the added complication of stress, fever, debility, general malaise and a high sedimentation rate triggering off the condition. In general, this implies a run-down condition which, when a certain point of weakness is reached, succumbs to an additional factor such as excessive fatigue, shock, or dampness.

Gouty Arthritis
It attacks men more than women, but can be found in both sexes in later years. It too is an acute form of arthritis and an excess of uric acid is also involved. Exposure to cold and damp and the use of some drugs and insulin or liver extract may initiate an attack. The excess of uric acid in gouty arthritis again implies a nutritional imbalance (excessive consumption of meat, meat products and other proteins, in particular), which must be permanently corrected to avoid recurrence of such attacks.

Acute rheumatism or arthritis in any form implies a previous history of abuse in one form or another, of imbalanced nutrition and stress. Hereditary influences may play a part – but the same mistakes in diet, habits and ways of living are usually perpetuated from one generation to another. Environment may alter – not always for the better – but the pressure of life is often greater and the quality less. The general value of food has certainly suffered a gradual decline over the years, providing less protection against disease. Drugs are more toxic and more readily used. Climatic conditions do not alter, though the ability to offset such conditions has improved. Hygiene and social conditions have demonstrated vast improvements over the last few decades. On balance, however, while people live longer, it is with a sub-standard level of health. This sub-standard level reduces resistance to disease and, when sufficient adverse influences coincide, acute attacks of disease take place. This is one of the reasons why rheumatism and other common ailments are more prevalent in the damp winter months.

These disorders do not arise overnight. The conditions for such an attack must have existed over a period – possibly for years – with previous mild attacks treated by aspirin or some analgesic or other. The gradual lowering of resistance, the accumulation of toxic products in the system (especially urates and uric acid in rheumatic disorders), and the persistent abuse of the natural reserves of the body, reach a point where it only requires one or more adverse condition to initiate an acute attack. This condition may be fatigue, exposure or damp. Unfortunately, it is usually this latter condition only, and not the previous history, which is blamed for the ailment.

Acute ailments are nature's warnings and when treated by natural methods, can often be used to advantage. Such methods include diet therapy, the permanent correction of dietetic errors, attention to postural and other defects in the musculoskeletal system and the avoidance of suppressive drugs which, while providing relief, do so at the expense of future health. Drugs, which undoubtedly save and prolong life in later years, should be only adopted when strictly essential. The habitual use of pain killers, stimulants, tranquillizers and sleeping pills can only be condemned, since all such drugs are toxic and hasten and complicate degenerative diseases.

Osteoporotic Bones

Osteoporosis, as has been previously mentioned, is a clinical condition where the bone becomes less dense and more brittle. Osteoporotic bones are a common danger in older people, particularly women, who tend to suffer more from the disease. Osteoporosis in women is often not evident until well after the menopause and even then may be associated with rheumatoid arthritis. The condition, however, does involve a serious risk of fractures.

During pregnancy, women may suffer a calcium loss resulting

in later osteoporosis. Calcium deficiency in the diet is the usual factor in the cause of osteoporosis. Pregnant women tend to suffer more, because any deficiency in the level of serum calcium must be made good by the removal of calcium in the bone. The avoidance of osteoporosis can be said to commence with correct nutrition and, in particular, full attention to calcium levels during pregnancies.

Osteoporosis can be a secondary feature of hyperthyroidism or other endocrine disorders. In general, however, osteoporosis is due to a calcium deficiency in the diet which has persisted for years. The two supplementary essentials in the diet are calcium and vitamin D. Three further essentials in the prevention of osteoporosis are mobility, physical activity and as much sunshine as possible.

Osteoporosis is, to a very large extent, one of the degenerative diseases which can be avoided. *One of the dangers of the corticosteroid drugs is that of aggravating or causing an osteoporotic condition.* In age, balance and the possibility of fractures become serious considerations and the risk of fracture is very much larger when osteoporosis is present.

Osteoporosis can cause a great deal of spinal pain, kyphosis of the spine and loss of height, but the greatest danger is fracture in the vertebrae or other bones. Manipulation is contra-indicated in the treatment of osteoporosis, but other gentle measures which increase circulation and nutrition of the affected parts are useful. While fatigue has to be avoided, mobility is essential and over-resting has to be avoided. A spinal support is necessary in advanced cases, but calcium and vitamin D supplements are essential. Again, however, prevention is better than cure and correct nutrition assumes a vital role in the prevention of this dangerous complication for the older person.

CHAPTER EIGHT

BRONCHITIS, EMPHYSEMA AND ASTHMA

The changes which take place during life should, in an orderly existence, be gradual. Greater benefit and a longer and more trouble-free life is assured when the transition from youth to middle and old age has been imperceptible at any one period. Gradual change permits time for adaptation and accommodation and allows reduced physical activity to be matched to reduced lung capacity and vice versa.

One of the changes in age is the stooping posture and the gradual loss of height due to shrinkage in the cervical discs. These changes limit mobility in the thoracic vertebrae and the thoracic cage. Kyphosis (forward bending of the upper spine) is very common, even among the not-so-old, when posture is poor. But few spines are normal and a combination of kyphosis, lumbar lordosis (where the spine moves inwards at the lower end of the spine) and scoliosis (lateral curvature of the spine) is frequently found.

Past history and the unity of the body should never be forgotten. This is often demonstrated in the shape, mobility and muscular power of the thoracic cage. Weight-bearing is centred on the powerful lumbar vertebrae, the sacro-iliac area and the hips. Great stress, therefore, is placed on this area, especially in obesity and in the tall person with a long spine. The lumbo-sacral area, therefore, is often the site of strain, rheumatic and lumbar pain and malposition. The same area is also involved in degenerative arthritic changes, hastened by the same stresses.

Similar degenerative changes take place in the cervical and thoracic area when habitual stooping, sedentary occupations and tension and lack of exercise restrict mobility in the ribs and neck. Low back pain, especially that resulting from a tilted pelvis and a 'short leg' – when one leg is shorter than the other – can cause a compensatory curve in the thoracic and cervical area, which then becomes a potential cause of headaches, fibrositis and restriction of mobility in those parts.

Heredity and Environment
Postural defects can commence early enough. Dietetic errors

commence even earlier. The future development of respiratory disease can have its origin in childish catarrhal 'snuffles'. Hereditary influences and environment have a larger influence on respiratory ailments than most complaints. Again, however, such influences are unnecessarily transmitted through ignorance and environment. If the same nutritional imbalance is perpetuated from one generation to another, the same result will almost inevitably ensue. Efforts to improve environment by better housing and less pollution must be matched by improvements in nutrition if early deaths or a difficult old age are to be avoided.

Environment has a profound effect upon respiratory disease. The chances of contracting chronic bronchitis and its sequela-emphysema – are four times greater in the damp industrial areas than in Southern England, and the so-called Black Country is black indeed. Hence the popularity of the drier and sunnier South-Eastern coastal districts of England, especially for the retired person, who can perhaps escape the worst effects of climate and industrialization.

While Britain has its own problems resulting from elderly migrants seeking more salubrious surroundings for their retirement, a similar process is being repeated in all Westernized countries. It is a process which will inevitably go unchecked as retirement ages are lowered and material resources increase.

That respiratory diseases like asthma, bronchitis, emphysema (and lung cancer), are largely due to the continued bombardment of the membranes and cells of the respiratory tract by irritants, is common knowledge. Atmospheric irritants can be – and are being – slowly reduced. It is doubtful, however, whether the best regulations can be truly effective while the end-products of sophisticated societies – cars, new chemical processes, and so on – continue to extend pollution in one form or another.

Added Disadvantages
Climate, atmospheric pollution and social conditions have always featured in the reasons given for respiratory ailments. But there are added disadvantages, including habitual poor posture, shallow breathing, irritation of mucous membrane arising from smoking, chemical sprays and fumes. Not all fumes and other aspects of pollution can be avoided. Public and commercial transport pollutes the atmosphere for all, especially in cities and

towns. Country districts do not entirely escape, since they occasionally suffer from the widespread spraying of crops with toxic chemicals. Also, most domestic aerosols are irritants to the lungs.

The effects of atmospheric pollution show up dramatically. Clean-air countries – the less populated and industrialized Scandinavian ones, for example – have a remarkably low incidence of bronchitis. Great Britain has the highest incidence of bronchitis in the world; 17 per cent of the male population between the ages of 40 and 60 are affected by it.

With all the geographical, environmental and industrial disadvantages to be considered, it becomes essential to eliminate as many other adverse factors as possible and to build up the resistance of the body. That this should commence at the earliest year in life is obvious. Unfortunately, the nutritional errors and chemical imbalance usually commence in childhood and are carried through to adult years.

The origin of most respiratory ailments is irritation of the mucous membrane of the respiratory tract and an excess of mucus-forming elements. It has already been noted that the mucus-forming foods are also acid-forming and, under modern methods of food production, contain chemicals which damage and irritate the tissues.

External irritants – smoke, dust, fumes, chemical sprays and nicotine, damp climate and lack of sun – cause havoc with the lungs. These adverse influences can be even more powerful when poor posture and restriction of the thoracic cage and lack of exercise, reduce the ventilatory capacity of the lungs.

Asthma: a Psychosomatic Ailment

Bronchitis invariably displays a previous history of catarrh and frequent colds. Chronic bronchitis terminates, as a rule, in emphysema. Asthma has the same causes, but with the difference that it is a psychosomatic ailment and the superimposed factors are allergy, stress and hereditary influences. Allergy, however, denotes a heightened sensitivity. This hypersensitivity can be reduced or even eradicated by correct nutrition and persistent efforts to relax. It can be a reaction to personal environment as well as a personal idiosyncrasy. All disease produces stress or tension and the ability to relax is a powerful asset in avoiding or limiting diseased conditions, but the necessity to relax is even more evident in psychosomatic ailments.

It has been previously noted that the average diet contains an excess of mucus-forming foods, especially the refined carbohydrates. Children fed on milk and on a starchy diet (often given too many sweets or chocolates), soon develop catarrhal snuffles, adenoids and enlarged tonsils. Colds develop easily, even in adults on such a diet, a sign that nature is seeking to eliminate excess mucus and other toxic matter. Colds, catarrh and minor chest complaints, which normally would quickly clear up by rest, warmth and abstention from solid food, are too often suppressed by toxic drugs.

Coughing: a Safety Valve

A continued imbalance in diet causes almost permanent catarrh and this condition tends to restrict the free use of the lungs. Shivering is a natural reaction to loss of body heat, a reflex some older people lose. The 'cough reflex' is not lost in the elderly. Coughing is a safety valve, in that it is nature's way of expelling irritants. Palliatives used to suppress coughs – particularly some patent drug preparations – do more harm than good.

Catarrh, of course, is not confined to the respiratory system. Mucous membrane contains cells which secrete mucus and it is found extensively throughout the body and lines all cavities connected directly or indirectly with the skin. Thus the respiratory tract, the alimentary tract and parts of the genito-urinary tract are lined with mucous membrane which secrete mucus. Irritation of the mucous membrane causes a variety of symptoms, depending upon the site of irritation. Nasal catarrh arises when the mucous membrane of the nasal passages is irritated; bronchitis when the irritation spreads to the bronchial passages. But a similar condition is found in dyspepsia, cystitis and acute catarrhal colitis. In the latter cases the irritant is normally traced to food or drink, with the added possibility of climatic conditions, fatigue or draught superimposed.

With colds and catarrh, however, though the conditions are somewhat the same, there is the added subjection to atmospheric irritants, fumes, sprays and dust and an overall picture of excessive intake of mucus-forming foods. The excess mucus created by diet and irritants, is simple catarrh in the first stages of a catarrhal cold, and is removed by coughing. The cough reflex, however, is not always sufficient to expel the mucus secreted. Unless the intake of irritants – whether from food or other irritants – is vastly reduced, the excessive secretion of mucus will continue and, because the cough reflex is insufficient to deal with the mass of mucus, there is a build-up of mucus in the lungs.

Symptoms of Bronchitis

Neglected or suppressed colds and catarrh lead to a recurrence of such attacks and, eventually, to bronchitis. Bronchitis is characterized by cough, breathlessness, slight fever, head cold, sore throat and muscular pain in the back. There is a muco-purulent discharge and the cough, though tiresome, is the essential mechanism for expelling the accumulated mucus.

Simple acute bronchitis is a relatively uncomplicated ailment which soon responds to rest, warmth and freedom from irritants. Three or four days' rest on non-solid food – preferably fruit juices, honey water and clear or thick onion soup – is often sufficient for the severe symptoms to subside. The cough reflex should be encouraged to ensure the expulsion of the offending mucus. When coughing becomes easier, usually after a day or two, the symptoms will gradually die down, though an acute attack of bronchitis can last from two or three weeks.

Postural drainage – namely lying over a bed or with cushions on a large chair without arms, with the head down and the weight supported by the folded arms on the floor – is a good method of expelling muco-purulent matter from the lungs. This position must be practised carefully. One minute is sufficient the first time, gradually increasing both the time and frequency when necessary.

Acute Bronchitis

Manipulation, chest packs and steam inhalations relieve congestion and speed recovery. Natural methods of treatment can do more to relieve and cure early chest complaints than any drug. What is more important is that natural methods are safe, with no side effects and no illusion of a rapid cure. One of the dangers of acute bronchitis is that it is possible to be deceived into thinking that the disease has completely abated, only to find within a short period that such is not the case.

Unfortunately, colds, catarrh and acute bronchitis are rarely accepted as warnings and, particularly when adverse climatic conditions, atmospheric pollution and errors in diet are unaltered, recurrent attacks of bronchitis ensue. The normal pattern is for eacn successive attack of bronchitis to become more severe and at shorter intervals. Chronic bronchitis is the inevitable result and chronic bronchitis cases rarely live to any great age.

The first attack of bronchitis should be accepted as a severe warning. Continued subjection to irritants, plus an excessively mucus-forming food intake, will more probably initiate further attacks. Unless the necessary changes are made, it is easy for chronic bronchitis to develop.

Older people can develop acute bronchitis, but their symptoms are not quite the same as younger people's. For example, breathlessness can be commonplace and rises in temperature are often absent. There is a dry cough and multiple rhonchi sounds in the chest. There is no reason why, when all irritants are removed and the conditions of rest and warmth maintained, older people should not recover in the same way as younger sufferers. Postural drainage is impossible for the weak, elderly person, but most active people between 60 and 70 can perform even a modified form of postural drainage.

There is no doubt that drugs may, at some time, be necessary for temporary treatment. But what is far more important is the need to prevent bronchitis.

Effects of Emphysema

Bronchitis, when it becomes chronic, usually terminates in emphysema, a condition where the alveoli or smaller bronchioles of the lungs suffer from over-distension. The walls of the finer bronchioles are stretched and thinned and rupture results in air sacs of varying sizes. The degenerative changes in the lungs lead to hyperinflation of the lungs, stretched and narrowed alveolar capillaries, and loss of elastic tissues. Persistent inflation causes increase in the size of the thoracic cage, while the vital capacity of the lungs is diminished, but the volume of air remaining in the lungs increases. This means a decrease in oxygen and an increase in the CO_2 tension.

Emphysema develops slowly and natural compensation does take place. In advanced cases, however, the enlargement of the chest, depressed diaphragm and dyspnoea on effort are obvious.

Bronchopneumonia in older people is often the result of debility, illnesses or accidents, causing enforced rest and stagnation of the bloodstream and reduced resistance. It is for such occasions that antibiotics should be reserved. Frequent and unnecessary recourse to antibiotics can reduce their efficacy just when they are essential.

Symptoms of Bronchial Asthma

Bronchial asthma is characterized by paroxysms of difficult breathing which recur at frequent intervals. In asthma there is a large allergic and nervous element. Stress emotion and subjection to some particular allergy aggravate or initiate the attack. The same irritants and excess of mucus-forming foods which create colds, catarrh and bronchitis, however, are also part of the cause of asthma.

Chronic asthma displays the same irritation of mucous membrane, the same excess of mucus and hyper-distension of the lungs, coughing and expectoration of mucus. In asthma, it is the expiratory movement of air that is impaired, due to narrowed passages and excessive secretion. Prolonged expiration, wheezing and gasping for breath are the familiar features of asthma.

Asthma tends to become chronic if not treated early. All external irritants must be avoided as much as possible and a near mucus-free diet adopted. Tension and emotional upsets must be avoided and the allergic element traced and avoided. To attempt to control asthma by the use of one of the countless ephedrine-based preparations is to ignore the cause. Sedatives and cough suppressors should always be avoided. All drugs have side-effects and anxiety, depression and tachycardia (rapid heart-beat) can result from ephedrine alone. The adreno-cortical steroid drugs should be used as a last resort.

Most respiratory diseases have simple origins. Accidents, environment, occupation and hereditary influences are an inseparable feature of life. To counter and minimize the effects of irritants, therefore it is essential to employ beneficent influences to the best advantage. The first tendency to colds, catarrh, adenoids, sinusitis, and so on, should be accepted as warnings of future respiratory trouble. On a balanced diet, with adequate exercise, sunshine, good posture and moderate freedom from irritants, an occasional cold or catarrhal condition could be a normal event causing little inconvenience.

Blessing in Disguise

A cold, with its rapid expulsion of morbid matter, can be a blessing in disguise. When treated by rest, warmth and abstention from solid food for a day or two, it can be even more of a blessing.

During a cold there is a natural loss of appetite. Nature has sufficient work on hand in countering the effects of the cold and eliminating mucus and other morbid waste matter which has accumulated in the system and reduced resistance to disease. Rest, warmth and diluted fruit juices or clear vegetable soups are the main requirements. Colds are a warning – they should not be suppressed by drugs.

Freedom from respiratory diseases, or from the worst effects of these diseases is, in age, a matter of past history. When, however, their first indication is shown in later years, there are many reasons for not assuming the worst. Providing previous health has been good, environmental or occupational risk has been limited and posture and mobility above average, then natural resilience will overcome normal attacks of bronchitis. Previous good health denotes a certain attention to diet and the avoidance of obesity and a higher level of resistance.

As always, prevention is better than cure. Where prevention is not entirely possible, limitation and the postponement of degenerative changes is the next objective. This can only be achieved when mobility, sound nutrition, good posture and moderation are established factors in life.

It is not always possible to select a favourable geographical position in which to work and live. Where, geographically, pollution and climate are very adverse, there is a necessity to be even more stringent about avoiding irritants, an excessive intake of mucus-forming foods and poor posture. Escape from the worst effects of pollution is all the more essential in later life, especially before natural resistance has become eroded by years of that pollution. Moving to a more salubrious area is an understandable desire, especially in the person subject to chest complaints. Earlier retirement, improved pensions and better planning and transport are slowly but surely offering increased opportunities in that direction.

CHAPTER NINE

POSTURE, RELAXATION AND BREATHING

Habitual good posture, the ability to relax, and correct breathing may be likened to a health insurance policy with accrued benefits. These benefits are amply demonstrated in the latter years of life, but they are not obtained without a certain amount of discipline, which, in itself, helps to form character.

It is very easy to slump when tired. To relax and let go is one thing − to droop is another. Relaxing and good posture both relieve tension. Correct breathing, by raising the supply of oxygen and removing carbon dioxide, also relieves tension. The nervous system demands a free flow of oxygen, like other parts of the body. Tension is part of living: it is safer and better to counteract it with the means nature supplies, rather than resort to toxic tranquillizers.

Erect posture does not mean the stiff carriage of a soldier on parade, nor does relaxing mean slumping in a chair. Good posture can be defined as: head up, chin in, chest up and out − not puffed out − shoulders high, abdomen in, legs and feet straight so that the body inclines slightly forward.

Methods of Relaxing

Relaxation can be induced, but it requires practice and patience. Yoga is extremely helpful as regards posture, breathing and relaxation. A simple method of relaxing, however, is to lie flat on the floor and let the arms and legs go absolutely limp, keeping the mind completely blank. It takes time to achieve the art of relaxing and the first necessity is to be conscious of tension and then of making no conscious effort to relax. Those who have to stand or sit for long periods should also try relaxing with the legs almost at right angles up against a wall or piece of furniture. The buttocks should be as near to the wall or furniture as possible, so that the legs are propped up at a good angle. This position should be maintained for a moment or two, relaxed by bending the knees, and repeated a second time. Where the circulation in the legs is poor, or varicose veins exist, the position with the legs up is particularly advised. The erect position has some disadvantages. Most can be avoided, but weight-bearing strains and gravity can be mitigated by correct posture, the ability to relax and spending a few moments on corrective positioning.

Oxygen and water are the first essentials of life. Few people make full use of their lungs, yet upon this depends the supply of oxygen to the bloodstream and the removal of carbon dioxide. Many headaches are caused simply by oxygen deficiency, though this is but a minor indication of the damage caused by shallow breathing. Inefficient use of the lungs can be equated to a nutritional deficiency, but the effects are much more rapid.

It should be remembered that the lungs are one of the means by which waste products are removed from the body, especially carbon dioxide. If balance is not maintained in the lungs – namely, if there is an oxygen deficiency and an excess of carbon dioxide – the results are soon obvious. But with shallow breathing, while the effects are lassitude, headache, irritability and tension, such effects are often commonplace and unconnected with unused lung capacity.

A Breathing Exercise

Diaphragmatic breathing can be included in relaxing, since the best place is either on the bed (the mattress, incidentally, should always be firm), or on the floor. Lie on the floor with the head slightly supported on a thin pillow and the knees raised a little. For the first few times place a book on the abdomen. On expiration the book should sink down as the abdominal muscles contract. By placing a hand on the book and pushing it into the abdomen, the abdominal muscles can be educated to contract during expiration. On inspiration the book should rise, as the abdomen rises with inspiration. With the next expiration the book should sink again, as the abdominal muscles contract.

Commence breathing exercise with gentle inspiration through the nose (blow the nose first in case of impediment), then noisily out through the mouth, emptying the lungs as much as possible.

Diaphragmatic breathing can be practised standing in front of a mirror. The exercise should be commenced the same way: clearing the nose, followed by a gentle inspiration and a noisy exhalation via the mouth. Stand in front of the mirror with the hands on each side of the lower ribs, the tips of the fingers pointing towards the centre line of the front of the chest. When exhaling, the fingers should be approximately in the centre of the chest. Almost at the end of expiration, gentle pressure should be exerted by the palms of the hands on the sides of the chest.

Inspiration through the nose follows the expiration and during this, the lower ribs should move outwards against the palms of the hands, forcing the fingertips apart.

Oxygen Starvation

Lack of energy, a frequent complaint of young and old, is attributed to everything except the real cause – an absence of oxygen. Listlessness due to oxygen starvation produces lassitude and fatigue, which is invariably reflected in a slumped posture. This cramps the abdominal tissues and restricts mobility in the chest, a constricting effect which reduces respiratory function and aggravates the original condition. Involuntary movements like yawning are indications of the need for oxygen.

Good posture, relaxing and deep-breathing are three essentials to continued mobility, nutrition of tissues, circulation and the reduction of tension. Each, in its own way, contributes to positive thinking, since each demands discipline, control of the mind or positive action.

Neglect of these essentials leads to oxygen deficiency, early degeneration and an additional burden upon digestion (from cramping the abdominal organs), and upon the nervous system. Like all other aspects of health, training in good posture, breathing and relaxation should commence at an early age and be maintained throughout life. It is an unfortunate fact, however, that such training, often habitual in the educative years, is soon forgotten or given up when commencing to earn a livelihood. But it is throughout adult life, especially when following a sedentary occupation, that it is all the more necessary to continue.

Deep Breathing

Tension, such a commonplace complaint, is reduced when posture is good and when relaxation is practised. What is not generally realized, however, is that deep breathing plays a valuable part in reducing tension. Years of tension wreak havoc with the nervous system and are implicated in the psychosomatic ailments – asthma, gastric and duodenal ulcers and a host of other common ailments.

The benefits accruing from good posture, the ability to relax and deep breathing are cumulative, in that they increase resistance to disease and delay degenerative changes. The neglect of these features proves cumulative, causing early degeneration, debility and weakened resistance. In effect, there is a weakening of the reserves that should be available in later life. Insurance (assurance) for health is not simply a matter of signing a policy and paying a premium.

Poor Posture

Inefficient use of the lungs is frequently combined with poor posture. The result, especially if nutrition is imbalanced and the body is subject to more than its share of irritants, is affliction of the lungs in one form or another. There can, however, be a half-and-half stage which will carry one through on a sub-normal standard of health, but which is not conducive to a ripe old age. A little more effort in previous past history would have raised the general standard of health and supplied improved prospects for enjoying retirement to the full.

A stooping posture in the earlier years, with all its contributing effects, limits the allowances that can be made in later life. The person who stoops at 40 will have anticipated his future body position by anything from 20 to 30 years or even more. What is more, he or she will use up some reserves of adaptation in lung efficiency, nervous energy and mobility as the years go by, leaving less for a later age. The more extensive the history of postural defects, lack of relaxation and oxygen deficiency becomes, the less are the opportunities for enjoying a long and healthy life.

Each year of delay in correcting faults in posture, relaxation and breathing adds to the earliest development of degenerative change. However, even when many years of delay have caused some irretrievable damage, improvement can be gained and the rate of degenerative change slowed down. Nature quickly responds to beneficial influences. A clean bloodstream and a free flow of nutriment to the tissues, reduces congestion and ensures the necessary interchange of chemicals upon which the cells depend. Even in middle and older age, there is ample room for improvement.

CHAPTER TEN

BALANCE AND MOBILITY

Breathlessness, lack of mobility and fatigue are common degenerative symptoms in age. The onset of such symptoms should be gradual. The adoption of balanced nutrition, moderation, posture and correct lung ventilation will delay degenerative changes. Accidents cannot be foreseen, environment may not be good nor hereditary influences helpful. Too much importance, however, can be attached to the latter. Most degenerative disorders are dictated by past history, which is more a personal matter than a by-product of previous generations. Accidents leave scarring and can be a focus for future degeneration. Many accidents, however, are the result of slow reflexes or lack of concentration. This unhappy state is all too common in people who have sub-normal health or habitually consume pain-killers, tranquillizers or other drugs.

Environment, as we have seen, also shapes the future, but some mitigation can also take place there. Past history affects the mental and physical future of every individual. In the main, however, the future depends upon work, discipline, moderation and a positive approach to life. Benefits are usually earned. Ageing is a continuous process, despite the fact that a severe crisis or illness may result in a sudden spurt in the process. This 'leap-frogging' in age does arise with varying effects, according to the severity of the crisis and the resilience of the individual.

Warning Signs of Imbalance

Few people go through life with no mishaps or crises. The obvious thing is to be physically and mentally equipped to the fullest possible extent so that the worst effects can be minimized and recovery made as complete as possible. Apart from accidents, unexpected stress or severe misfortune, nature usually supplies warning signs of imbalance or 'dis-ease'. These signs normally take the shape of the many common acute ailments that afflict sophisticated societies. When such indications of disease are repeatedly suppressed or ignored, chronic disease must ensue – hastening degenerative changes and shortening the life-span.

Exceptions to the rule always exist. A few active old people have defied practically every health law and lived to advanced ages with no crippling effects and no serious disease. Such examples, few though they are, frequently form the basis for much opposition to the obvious need for exerting discipline and moderation in the mode of life. Serious thought, however, will usually demonstrate that the people concerned have possessed both special qualities of resilience and an exceptional aptitude for enjoying life, combined with positive (and sometimes selfish) attitudes. The truth, of course, is, that such examples are put forward, not as strict evidence, but as an excuse for not applying discipline and moderation.

Life can never be equal, nor attitudes alike. No one can expect, therefore, that ageing, inevitable though it may be, can be uniform. Nature dictates the pattern, but not the pace. The pace is only dictated by the deliberate or unwitting breaking of natural laws. Even the fact that ageing in different parts of the body may be unequal, can be due to past history – accidents, previous illness, abuse or misuse – or inherent weakness. One factor, however, is constant. Normal health and the delay of real old age can only be expected when sufficient attention has been paid to the issues governing health and resistance to degeneration. The more attention that is paid to these factors – without attention being converted to obsession – the greater the benefits in the latter age of life.

First Indications of Ageing

Faulty posture, reduced mobility, breathlessness on exertion and fatigue are among the first indications of ageing. Reactions and accommodation to positional changes are slowed down. These changes, which should be slow, can be accelerated by shock or fear. It is for these very reasons that balance assumes such importance to the older person.

The thinning of the intervertebral discs produces loss in height. Weight-bearing tends to shift because of degenerative changes in the skeletal system. These bony changes produce a tendency to stooping and make balancing more difficult. Good posture can be maintained till very late in life. Poor posture throughout life means poorer posture in later years. Where good posture has been a habit for years, it tends to remain. In age, mental processes and reactions may slow down, but years of habit are very resistant to change.

Postural Hypotension

Reduced accommodation to positional changes also results from interrupted or reduced blood-supply to the brain. Postural hypotension causing a little dizziness or limpness on reaching the vertical position from sitting or lying in bed is quite common. Almost one out of every ten older people present this symptom. Where the blood pressure is low, or where it is subject to rapid changes, this can arise with alarming frequency. Anaemic subjects are the most likely victims and balanced nutrition and possible addition of food supplements is essential.

Postural hypotension can cause very disturbing vertigo or even fainting. People of mature age who have a tendency in this direction should always rise slowly and carefully from a chair or bed, avoid quick, jerky movements, straining at stool or hot baths. Older people should, in any case, avoid hot baths and be content with the safer and less enervating warm bath only.

Low and high blood-pressure can cause difficulties in balance. Sudden kinking of the vertebral arteries from jerky movements, especially when the arteries have hardened and blood-pressure is high, is another cause of vertigo. Those subject to these disturbing symptoms should take care to avoid jerky movements and, where high blood-pressure and arterio-sclerosis is present, tight collars or any restriction of the neck should be avoided. At no age should garments ever restrict circulation, but older people need to exert more care.

Drugs Cause Vertigo

Vertigo is a very unpleasant and frightening disorder. The sensation of instability and rotation in space saps confidence and discourages activity. It can arise from middle ear disease or wax in the ears and be a sign of a long history of catarrh. Drugs, unfortunately, often cause vertigo. A long history of taking quinine preparations, salicylate or barbiturate drugs often causes it. Hypersensitivity to such drugs will frequently cause vertigo, and there is no doubt that the more drugs can be avoided in earlier life, the greater the freedom from problems of balance in old age. For the same reason catarrh should be avoided; this is largely a nutritional problem, mainly connected with an excessive intake of refined and denatured carbohydrates.

Instability in the elderly can arise from a variety of causes. The first serious fall, especially in the person who lives alone, can be a heavy blow to morale and confidence. The fear of recurrence does nothing to encourage the mobility that is essential to maintain free movement and strength in limbs and a good blood supply to all parts of the body. Elderly people require to make purposeful movements which allow time for positional changes and take account of the shift in weight-bearing.

The habit of good posture, relaxation and correct breathing brings untold advantages in later life, in that it delays many of the degenerative changes and reduces their impact when they do arise. Even normal sight and hearing can retain a high efficiency in age, when moderation and a balanced nutrition have been effective for some years. Defective sight and hearing are not conducive to good balance.

Balance, with its well-known risk of fracture if upset, is affected by so many factors. Obesity, with its resultant descent of the abdominal organs, poor posture, weight-bearing stress and additional burden on the feet, is an obvious handicap. A great many falls are due to a combination of weight and weakened foot structure alone. Obesity causes so many problems that the strain on the feet tends to be overlooked.

Chiropody is Essential

Distorted and 'buckled' joints in the feet are more common in women than in men. For all that, the big toes of both men and women are often the first joints to show degenerative changes. Painful feet and weak ankle joints can easily cause imbalance, but when this is aggravated by excessive weight or poor posture, or a combination of both, balance becomes more precarious. The feet should never be neglected and chiropody is even more essential in age, despite the reduced strain occasioned by decreased activity.

Mobility is vital at any age. Fears of imbalance, difficult movement, breathlessness and painful feet are the main reasons put forward for restricted mobility. But prolonged rest causes stagnation, lack of nutrition to tissues, stiffened joints and weak muscles. It is very easy to set up a vicious circle where the avoidance of movement decreases the ability to move. Too much bed or chair rest is a great danger to health.

Mobility is important for a hundred and one reasons. Safety can depend upon being mobile. It is, however, also important for social and family reasons. The ability to play with grandchildren gives extreme satisfaction. Young children are quite happy to *toddle* along with grandparents. Adolescents, however, can be patronizing to slower elders. It is the married progeny – pressed for time – who say, 'Don't bother, father, you're too slow', or 'I'll do that, mother, you just sit down.' The latter can be said either with good intent or with the obvious inference that the older person will be a handicap. For the maintenance of good family relationships, therefore, it is worth the effort to remain fully active. So much family enjoyment can be unnecessarily lost by being under-active in earlier years.

Pains Have Rheumatic Origin

The influence of mobility and circulation is made manifest hundreds of times in the course of life. Most people, at one stage or other, suffer from muscular pains and joint stiffness. The vast majority of such pains have a rheumatic origin: aggravated by damp, unaccustomed exercise or fatigue. The presence of uric and other acids in the system from imbalanced nutrition and an imbalance in the elimination of waste products, do, of course, add to the pain and stiffness of locomotion. These pains, most noticeable on rising, ease off during the day when the circulation is stimulated and the joints are loosened by exercise or activity.

Degenerative changes add to the complications of stiffened joints and weakened muscles. More determined effort to maintain mobility is required as age progresses. While stiffened joints are not necessarily more painful, pain is a frequent complication, especially on movement. Mobility requires more effort in age and energy requires oxygen. Postural changes and degeneration constrict the chest and lung capacity is reduced. Breathless on effort, therefore, is a more frequent hindrance to mobility. When fears of imbalance are added to the stiffness and shortness of breath there is an understandable desire to reduce mobility, especially if movement of a joint or limb causes pain.

Guarding Vulnerable Limbs

The ability to endure pain is a very variable factor – even the threshold of pain differs from person to person. While, in general terms, a disciplined and strong character will withstand pain much better than a weaker and less intellectually endowed person, such is not always the case. There are times when it is preferable not to be blessed (or cursed) with imagination! Real or imagined pain produces a guarding of the affected part, especially joints or limbs which are under voluntary control. With age, this 'guarding' tends to become more pronounced.

What have to be avoided at all costs are the permanent muscular contractions, deformities and muscular wasting that can arise from maintaining a joint in a fixed position to avoid pain. Guarding can easily result in fixation, with all its difficulties and permanent disability, if it is carried to excess. Movement, in many joint diseases, may be painful, but short periods of pain are preferable to fixation and immobility.

The knees are highly susceptible to swollen joints and degenerative bone and muscle changes. A simple but effective exercise is to sit firmly in a chair which is high enough to allow the feet to just clear the ground. From this position the lower limbs can be swung from the knees without any weight-bearing stress. The movements should commence gently, swinging just an inch or two without a forced movement. Gradually the arc of the swing should be extended as movement becomes freer.

Similar types of movement can be adopted for the hip, where the whole leg is swung from the hip joint. In this case, a firm stand should be made on the stable leg and the body supported between two strong pieces of furniture, or the wall and a piece of furniture. Each leg should be exercised in turn. The arms, elbows, wrist, shoulder joints, can all be moved and exercised while sitting. Such movements should be slow and deliberate but have as fluid and rhythmic a character as possible.

It is surprising how much free movement can be restored or maintained when a deliberate policy of exercise is carried out. Patience and time are the essentials. There is no need to risk either imbalance, shortness of breath or fatigue. The periods of exercise should tend to be short, frequent and always commenced by gentle movement. Jerky and erratic movement should be avoided.

Exercising the Neck
The neck is particularly prone to stiffness in age. This arises from degenerative change, postural defects and tension. Quick and jerky movements of the head on the neck can, it has been noted, cause vertigo, faintness and loss of balance. Mobility in the neck area, however, is essential for the blood supply to the brain and to the deferment of degeneration. Freedom of movement in this area supplies economy of effort in that, so long as it is available, the head only need be turned to look sideways or backwards (as in reversing a car). Immobility in that area involves the entire trunk of the body in the turning movement.

Mobility can be kept relatively active if the neck is exercised sufficiently. Even younger people are advised to carry out neck and head exercises from a sitting position and with slow, deliberate but fluid movements. Such exercises should take the form of rolling the head, first clockwise then anticlockwise, side-bending it in both directions (tipping first to the right, then to the left), and by nodding movements of the head.

Emphasis must be placed on the fact that *all head and neck movements should be slow, deliberate and as fluid as possible*. Should any giddiness arise from any of the movements, then the exercises should be stopped and repeated with even more care at a later interval. Where conditions in the neck have been allowed to deteriorate, only small movements may be possible in the initial stages. With time and patience, however, increased mobility will be attained.

The head and neck are intimately concerned with balance. To ignore difficulty in movement in this area is to invite early problems of balance. The neck region is particularly prone to tension, postural defects and spinal anomalies. Most of these conditions respond to manipulation and can be corrected in earlier years. Even in later years, when, because of bony changes – inflammation of the vertebrae or possible bone emaciation – manipulation is contra-indicated, neuro-muscular treatment is beneficial.

Manipulation and physiotherapy are largely neglected in the battle against joint, muscle and nerve degeneration. There is no doubt that a great deal of the bony and neuro-muscular degeneration that arises in people can be both deferred and minimized by a combination of effective physical treatment and controlled exercise. The same treatment will aid the continuance of balance and effective nutrition.

Balancing Difficulties

Where difficulties in balance do exist, the emphasis must be on slower and more deliberate movements, especially on rising either from bed, a sitting position or the lavatory. All chairs should have stout arm rests, a firm high back and a firm base and the lavatory should have wall bars to assist rising. When getting up from a chair a firm grip should be taken on the arm rests and the feet should be placed well back under the chair before rising, so that the centre of gravity is maintained.

Faulty balance, breathlessness, pain or stiffness must never be allowed to interfere with mobility. Aids to locomotion – a stick or a walking aid – may be necessary in later life. Both are preferable to immobility. Even when bed-rest is necessary – and it should never be over-prolonged – exercises can be carried out and the limbs moved as much as possible to avoid weakness and stiffness. Prolonged inactivity produces severe stagnation and endangers life.

The inclination to 'stay put' can be very strong in the elderly. After all, there is very little inducement to move when the fear of imbalance is added to the other factors. Mobility, therefore, has to be preserved and encouraged. Relatives or misguided friends who encourage too much rest are performing a disservice that is highly detrimental, both physically and mentally. The normal person, even in extreme age, prefers to be independent and active. Given normal conditions, a healthy background and balanced nutrition, activity can be maintained. Like all good things in life, however, activity and mobility require some care and not a little effort.

CHAPTER ELEVEN

CONSTIPATION, DIARRHOEA, INCONTINENCE AND CYSTITIS

Constipation is an almost universal bugbear of mature and older people. It is, quite often, an unnecessary major worry. In the first place, a reduction in the quantity of food consumed, which should be automatic when energy output is reduced from lessened activity, would mean a normal reduction in faecal matter. Decreased activity and a reduction in peristaltic movement of the bowels, which is part of ageing, produces a tendency to constipation in older people. In age, therefore, while a daily movement of the bowels should normally take place, this is not truly essential. Bowel movements can be separated by 36 or 48 hours, without any ill-effect, providing that balanced nutrition and reasonable activity is maintained.

The bowels are one of the main organs in the process of eliminating waste toxic products from the body. Imbalance in the process of elimination means that other organs of elimination – the skin, lungs and kidneys – tend to become overburdened and that waste products accumulate in the system. One of the first results of constipation is headache, lassitude and – in younger people – acne and other skin troubles. Persistent imbalance in the elimination of waste products eventually causes many of the common ailments. It is rarely suspected, however, that imbalance in nutrition can be the major cause of imbalance in the process of elimination and the retention of waste products in the body.

Aperients and purgatives stimulate or irritate the bowels and cause an unnatural expulsion of faecal matter. Over-stimulation or irritation, however, weakens the natural mechanism. An occasional aperient will do little harm. It is when aperients and purgatives are used too frequently that damage to natural function becomes inevitable. People who are obsessed with the idea that a bowel action must take place at least once a day are those who create either the very condition originally feared or cause chronic diarrhoea. It is very rare, too, that such people really consider the role of diet in relation to a costive condition.

The Digestive Process

Food is first masticated, the salivary glands producing ptyalin, the salivary juice that helps to transform starches into sugar. This process continues after the food has been swallowed and enters the stomach. When the food has been in the stomach for about thirty minutes, the salivary action is checked by the acid of the gastric juices and the next stage in the digestive process begins. Two substances in the gastric juice – pepsin and rennin – further break down the food consumed. Other substances are involved in the breaking down of food material. The combined action of the whole gastric juices and the churning action of the muscular walls of the stomach mixes up and breaks down the food into a gravel-like consistency. At this stage the pyloric valve at the lower end of the stomach opens and permits a small quantity of the partially digested food to enter the duodenum – the first nine or ten inches of the small intestine.

Intestinal digestion begins when the softened food enters the bowels, where it is subject to the action of bile, pancreatic juice, intestinal juice and bacteria. Bile is made in the gall-bladder and liver and assists the digestion of fats; but it also contains some waste products removed from the blood. The pancreatic juice is concerned with the digestion of fats, starch and protein. Enzymes in the intestinal juice further act upon the food, and the bacteria in the small and large intestines play an important role in the latter part of digestion, being active in the fermentation and putrefaction of food.

Peristaltic Movement

Food material is continuously squeezed along the small and large intestine by peristaltic or wave-like motion. At intervals, mass peristalsis, a concentrated and enlarged form of movement, occurs. Continuous with this process of breaking down and movement is the absorption and assimilation of nutriment, the concentration of waste matter from the food and the liver and the reduction of liquid matter. The end result is the normal 'stool', which is dependent upon the food consumed, condition of the liver, manufacture of the vitamin B-complex in the intestinal bacteria, a sufficient intake (though not excessive) of liquid, and the total gastric juices. Exercise and tone in the abdominal muscles also play a vital role. Obesity causing visceroptosis – dropped abdominal organs – endangers bowel movement.

Reduction in the gastric juices is fairly frequent in age. It can be due to anaemia or to a deficiency of the B-complex vitamins, iron and calcium. Alternate diarrhoea and constipation and loss of appetite may result from these deficiencies. Balanced nutrition, therefore, does much to insure healthy bowel movement by providing the chemical ingredients for that action.

The necessity for less bulk and the inability to digest a great deal of roughage has already been outlined in the section on diet. Since activity, digestion, absorption and assimilation decline with age, so the appetite should correspondingly decline. Obesity, a menace at any time, is even more menacing in age, when problems of weight-bearing, visceroptosis, stagnation, posture and activity exert increased influence upon bowel movements.

Laxative Foods

The diet outlined will, in time, help to correct obesity and encourage a bowel activity where it has been deficient. Persistent constipation can be rectified even in later life, but it will take more time and patience. In addition to the diet outlined, there should be an emphasis on the laxative foods and food supplements. Vitamin B-complex, iron and calcium should be taken. The laxative foods advised for older people, especially those who are unable to tolerate bran, coarse wholemeal bread or coarse vegetables, are prunes, beetroot, mushroom, spinach (in small quantities), sunflower oil, agar-agar and black molasses. The latter two can be taken neat – at least one dessertspoonful a day – or dissolved in water.

Where there has been a long history of constipation, with its inevitable retention of waste products and disruption of natural bowel movement, an enema or two may be necessary in the initial stages. The water injected should be at blood heat and it can contain a little garlic oil (garlic is a good antiseptic), diluted soft soap or a little sunflower oil. The water should be retained as long as possible to soften the hard, impacted matter contained in the bowel.

Defaecation can be a difficult problem for the elderly. While in normal life there should be a certain pattern in bowel movement by setting a specific time – usually after breakfast – this should apply even more in later life, to combat forgetfulness. An established habit becomes difficult to break, the more so as years go by. Even if no bowel action results at the specific time, it should still be maintained. Another important factor for people of all ages, is the necessity for a natural 'squatting' position to facilitate bowel movement. A stool at least six inches high should be placed in the toilet and the knees raised on this when attempting a bowel movement which, incidentally, should never be forced.

There is a certain amount of strain and muscular effort when defaecating. Older people should be especially careful not to strain, and to adopt the squatting position. This is even more imperative when high blood-pressure or postural hypotension (inclination to fainting or temporary loss of consciousness), exists.

Unity of Body

One of life's lessons is the complete unity of the body. Apart from balanced nutrition and the avoidance of obesity, the importance of deep breathing and strengthening the abdominal musculature cannot be over-emphasized. Good posture and avoiding abdominal restriction is also essential. Obesity, weakness in the abdominal wall, and constipation are potent factors in causing femoral and other hernias of the groin in both men and women. Heavy lifting or over-stretching may precipitate the rupture, but weakness in the abdominal musculature is the first link in the chain of events leading to it.

Diarrhoea arises in all ages – young and old – and the causes are usually the same. Dietetic indiscretions – even the sudden eating of too much unaccustomed fruit – will cause diarrhoea, while an artificial diarrhoea is often induced by purgatives. Liquid paraffin is an irritant which the bowels must expel. As a remedy for constipation it should be avoided at all costs, since it also extracts protective elements from the tissues.

Acute diarrhoea, like acute gastro-enteritis, is largely caused by the necessity to expel some irritant or other. This can be caused by injudicious feeding, food poisoning or from drugs or metals. Antibiotics, salicylates, arsenic, lead and mercury all cause acute diarrhoea. The character and severity of the acute condition will depend upon the extent and duration of the irritant. It arises suddenly with abdominal cramp, malaise, loss of appetite and vomiting. The loss of fluid in possibly both directions must be rectified by ample fluids. The urgent treatment is rest, warmth, abstention from solid food and the replacement of lost liquid with warm honey and water, rice or barley water and clear vegetable soup. Apple or·grape juice can be given, but other fruit juices should be withheld.

In acute diarrhoea, like chronic diarrhoea, there is also usually a history of catarrh, superimposed upon the other factors. An imbalanced diet containing an excess of mucus-forming foods produces an excess of mucus in the body. Catarrh in the gastric system frequently causes diarrhoea, because very little additional irritant in the way of food or drug is necessary to initiate the attack.

Chronic diarrhoea, however, apart from its catarrhal aspect, is· often a symptom of disease elsewhere in the body and a thorough investigation is required into possible causes. Anaemia, liver disorders and malfunction of the thyroid gland are often accompanied by persistent diarrhoea.

Incontinency

Frequent micturition can be a serious problem at any age. Older people tend to accept it with resignation as one of the minor problems of age. Degeneration, lessened reflexes, pressure on the bladder from visceroptosis and interference from spinal anomalies and bad posture all influence bladder troubles. However, modern aids for both day and night incontinence are obtainable from surgical appliance stores, and can save much embarrassment – ·and work. Old people afflicted with incontinence should be encouraged to adopt these aids.

In the earlier adult years women are more prone to what is termed 'stress incontinence'. This weakness can continue throughout life, especially in nervous people who are easily upset or subject to tension. Coughing, lifting or straining can cause the involuntary flow. Dribbling incontinence is not always associated with stress incontinence, but is very frequent in younger people. Paradoxically, incontinence arises when there is chronic urinary retention due to obstruction of the urethra in the male or to a lack of nerve control. An enlarged prostate is the most common cause of bladder troubles in males over 60 years of age, though it is not uncommon in men under that age.

Ill-effects Not Inevitable

Enlargement of the prostate gland in males is not a necessary development, despite the frequency with which it occurs. Even when it does arise and surgical intervention becomes necessary, the vast improvements in surgery have made the operation an infinitely less dreaded occasion.

The prostate gland can be enlarged and produce no ill-effects providing the enlargement causes no obstruction to urinary flow. Natural degeneration, as age progresses, can actually reduce the incidence of prostate enlargement with all its attendant difficulties. Difficulty in voiding urine and 'dribbling incontinence' in older males is so common that there exists a danger of accepting such a condition as normal for age.

Bladder weakness alone can reduce the inclination of older people – men and women – to venture outdoors in the colder months. While some form of incontinence or bladder weakness is probably inevitable in the really old, there is no reason, apart from accident or nerve degeneration, why it should become seriously incommoding, though more difficulty would be experienced in the winter months.

Little is known about why the prostate gland should enlarge. It is a curious fact, however, considering that the prostate is concerned with the 'seed of life', that the seeds and kernels in nature exert a beneficial influence upon the gland. Pumpkin seeds, sunflower seeds and the germ of wheat, all help to maintain the health of the gland. Males over 50 are well advised to include such items in their diet.

An enlarged prostate does not necessarily mean urinary obstruction, but the symptoms of obstruction – dribbling, incontinence, difficulty in flow of urine, retention of urine or the presence of blood in the urine – would indicate the likelihood of enlarged prostate.

The danger that exists from urinary retention is infection of the kidneys. Catheterization also requires the utmost care to avoid infection. Vaginal and urethral douches can hardly be recommended for this very reason. The risk of infection is greater with females who carry douching to extremes.

Many of the problems connected with the genito-urinary tract are catarrhal in origin, a result of the tract's subjection to irritants, interference with nutrition and nerve supply, imbalanced diet and imbalance in elimination. Constipation, for example, can exert pressure effects upon the bladder while, at the same time, throwing an extra burden on the kidneys' role in the elimination process.

Cause of Cystitis

Cystitis, or inflammation of the bladder, a complaint quite frequent among females, is often basically a catarrhal condition, aggravated by cold, damp, prolapse of the womb, prolonged resting in bed and inadequate emptying of the bladder. Cystitis can be a secondary condition in infection from adjacent organs, such as the rectum or urethra. Enlargement of the prostate gland and the presence of stones in the bladder may contribute to cystitis. Obesity, which leads to visceroptosis and inactivity, has many inherent dangers in age and cystitis is one of the common problems emanating from it. In acute cystitis the symptoms are frequency, a burning sensation during urination and the presence of blood in the urine.

Cystitis can be avoided by existing on a balanced diet, avoiding an excess of mucus-forming foods, highly seasoned dishes or sauces, and moderation in alcohol. At the same time, however, good posture, deep breathing and the necessity to avoid obesity are paramount requirements. The latter ensure the tone, strength and integrity of the abdominal organs and muscles and form one of the best assurances against diseases of the genito-urinary system and bowel weakness.

Treatment for Cystitis

The common treatment for cystitis is by analgesic drugs and sedatives. In severe cases bladder irrigations are used. In all cases plenty of liquid is advised. Warmth, rest (not prolonged rest), and frequent drinking of parsley tea, rice, barley or oatmeal water can minimize or reduce the effects of cystitis. Hot fomentations to the abdomen provide some relief.

Lethargy and a too-ready acceptance of physical discomfort and disease is not confined to the old. It frequently commences in early adult life and predisposes to early degeneration of the functions of the body. Past history inevitably dictates future events. No one can pretend that the difficulties and embarrassments of age do not exist – they are hard physical facts. To hasten or increase these difficulties by neglecting simple rules of health and nutrition is unintelligent. Fortunately, even after many years of neglect, nature can respond to beneficial changes. Youth has no monopoly on recuperation and recovery, providing irretrievable mechanical damage has not occurred.

CHAPTER TWELVE

TREATMENT FOR THE OLDER PERSON

The changing conditions imposed by age necessitate a different approach in therapy. Such differences, however, are not imposed so much by age itself, as the clinical condition presented by that person. A sauna, for instance, which is normally suitable for most people up to 60 or 65, should not even be given at a much earlier age if there are symptoms of hypertension or heart disorder. It can be given for hypertension providing that the blood-pressure is not too high, and if the required attentive and skilled supervision is available.

The older person who displays degenerative symptoms should not ever be subjected to extremes of heat and cold, as in a sauna, without proper supervision. In most cases it will be contra-indicated. (The same applies to manipulative therapy. No reputable practitioner would ever use unnecessary force. X-rays will reveal if any osteoporosis or other bone condition prohibit manipulative therapy.)

A sauna should be interspersed and concluded with a cold shower, and is more effective if the head and back of the neck are kept cool by frequent changes of cold, wet towels to that area. If the head is kept cold and the concentration of blood in the cranial region reduced, body sweating can be safely increased. *The cold wet towels to head and neck are additional to the cold showers.*

Exercises and Physiotherapy

Advancing age and degenerative changes do not preclude either manual therapy, hydrotherapy, or even fasting. Account has to be taken of what is often termed 'fair wear and tear', but which, more often than not, is really 'unfair wear and tear'. Other than that, enormous benefit can be gained by neuro-muscular and other types of specialized physical treatment. Physiotherapy and exercises are not sufficiently adopted in combating degenerative changes. Too often the physiotherapy departments of hospitals are either grossly understaffed, or the older patient is unwilling to continue with the exercises and other therapies which would assist.

It has been conclusively proved that limbs can be strengthened and given a much larger range of movement, even in the very old. It is, however, when stiff and painful joints first arise that corrective exercises and physiotherapy should be instituted. In most cases the loss of mobility and muscular power is a relatively slow process and there is ample time for rejuvenation.

In treating older people, great care has to be taken to show interest, sympathy and a genuine desire to improve the condition. Any hint that treatment is achieving little, or is possibly a waste of time, will discourage effort. Pain may result from moving stiffened limbs; with due encouragement, this pain will normally be borne. A positive attitude on the part of the therapist and the older person being treated is vital. The importance of mobility, good posture and the fullest possible use of the lungs can never be over-emphasized.

Age is no bar to treatment. Manipulation in its wider and more general sphere can do a great deal to maintain and restore mobility and increase muscular strength. This applies to all manner of degenerative changes, from arthritis and chest complaints to many heart disorders and other malfunctions of the circulatory system.

Mobility Checks Degeneration

Exercising should not cease with age, though activity of any sort should never be pushed beyond the point of fatigue. The fact is, however, that sluggishness, obesity and lack of exercise will bring the point of fatigue much nearer. By gradually increasing the volume of exercise the heart, lungs and muscles can be strengthened so that the points between fatigue are extended. This can be achieved even where there is some limitation of movement from arthritic changes in the joints. Full movement in a joint may never be restored, or limitation prevented. The important factor, nevertheless, is to maintain as much mobility as possible in the spine, joints and rib cage. Mobility slows down degeneration in all parts of the body by increasing the blood flow and interchange of chemicals in the body.

Previous mention has been made of the need for exercises and that, in age, such exercises should be slow, deliberate and fluid. Stretching the limbs and relaxing tensed muscles can be achieved with very little effort. Where imbalance is a problem, care has to be taken to be securely positioned before attempting larger movements such as arm or leg swinging, but a great number of these exercises can be carried out when lying on the bed. The spine can be exercised while on the bed by simple trunk-raising movements. These exercises should be carried out in the prone position. In each case the head and lower parts of the body should be raised and lowered without forcing.

Exercise for Breath and Limb Control

An exercise which combines both breathing and limb movements is as follows: lie on the floor, face upward and stretch the arms backwards to their fullest extent. Commence by clearing the nose and breathing in gently through the nose and out through the mouth. Breathe out through the mouth, at the same time raising the legs and bringing the arms down to the side. Then breathe in through the nose, raising the arms up and back and, at the same time, lowering the legs. The legs must be kept as straight as possible *and lowered to within six inches of the floor only*.

The exercise must be repeated several times, breathing out, raising the legs and lowering the arms; breathing in, raising the arms and lowering the legs.

Some difficulty in co-ordination may be initially experienced. There will also be difficulty in keeping the legs straight and not completely lowered to the floor. It is best to limit the exercise to a few attempts only in the beginning and master the co-ordination required. By gradually increasing the exercise from two to five minutes greater proficiency and muscular strength is gained. The exercise should be relatively slow and deliberate and, if necessary, can be carried out on the bed.

Relatives looking after an older person should first master the exercise for themselves. Once this is achieved, slow, patient and deliberate demonstration should be given before the older person attempts it. From then on, depending upon age and condition, it is a question of very slow improvement. Progress may be limited to two or three movements at a time and in no instance should the older person be allowed to become exhausted. Incomplete movements are better than no movement and it is not wise to insist upon the full completion of any movement. Age is no bar to re-education of muscles and joints, which – even in younger age-groups – can sometimes be a lengthy process and involves a gradual extension of range of movement over a period of time.

Free Movement

The most important thing for the older person is free movement.

Where movement is limited, efforts must be made to either increase movement or retain the mobility that exists. All exercise, however, should be deliberate, free from any risk of imbalance and repeated at frequent and regular intervals. Spasmodic exercising producing fatigue should be avoided.

The stooping position and bad posture, which creates so much restriction, visceroptosis and faulty lung mechanics, can be alleviated by simply stretching the limbs and literally forcing the trunk erect. A completely erect position may not be possible, but the attempt should always be made. A high-backed chair can be used when balance is easily lost. Push the lower part of the spine as far back as possible and then stretch the arms upwards and straighten the spine to the maximum extent. This releases tension and encourages the flow of blood.

Frequent changes in position, even small movements, are vital. The stimulus to the circulation and oxygen supply helps to maintain body warmth. Extra clothing is no substitute for mobility.

Temperature Changes
Decreased accommodation to temperature changes in age require additional care. The extremes of heat and cold, which can be tolerated in young and adult life, are not advised in the later years. Slight variations are permitted but, in general, the temperature of the bath water should never be above 105°F. (40°C.) or below 90°F. (32°C.). The temperature of the bathroom itself must not be too low and some form of heating (preferably a radiator), is essential in the winter months.

The skin is one of the main organs of elimination. Neglect of the skin in earlier life is one of the factors in skin degeneration and the appearance of unsightly blemishes. Skin function and appearance depends upon balanced nutrition and balance in the process of elimination, intelligent exposure to air and sun and friction to the skin. Restrictive clothing prevents air movement on the skin surface.

Immobility causes stagnation. Immunity from such complications as oedema of the lungs and limbs, thrombo-embolism, constipation and bed sores depends upon restoring mobility at the earliest possible moment. The first consideration is to get the old person sitting up and then taking a few steps at a time to restore confidence and morale.

In serious illness, of course, the old person will undoubtedly be hospitalized. But there are a great many minor and chronic ailments for which home care is the best solution. Bed sores can only be prevented by good nursing and by encouraging the patient to move the limbs while in bed. Movement is essential to allow changes of position to relieve the sacral area, the buttocks, elbows and heels which are the main sites of bed sores. The weight of bed clothes should be reduced by a cradle at the bottom of the bed. Blanket baths or tepid wash downs should be given at least once a day. The bedroom should be warm when bed-clothes have to be removed to give the blanket bath. If possible, a second helper should be present.

Light, Gentle Massage

Abdominal massage reduces distension in that area, helps retain muscle tone and encourages bowel activity. Gentle massage with warm oil can be applied to the entire body if circumstances permit. The massage should be light, directed towards the heart when the limbs are involved, and in a circular (clockwise) direction when massaging the abdomen. With the patient sitting or propped up, massage of the chest or breathing exercises, or both, should be instituted at the first possible moment.

There are obviously moments when keeping the old person in bed may appear to entail less work for the helper. But this is neither a wise nor kind decision and can certainly shorten the life of the elderly person involved. Retention of mobility works to the advantage of both parties.

The normal warm (not hot) bath can be converted to a therapy by using a friction glove or brush while in the bath. A variation of this can be to place a bowl of common salt on a convenient ledge. Dip the wet hand into the salt and rub the skin with the wet salt. The friction or salt rub improves the tone of the skin. Further improvement can be gained by using a coarse towel for drying purposes.

Where movement is limited, help should be sought in taking baths. There should be few cases these days where no help is· forthcoming. What is most important, however, is to retain the mobility and independence that self-care can achieve. The importance of safety aids in the bathroom must never be over-looked. Even if they are not strictly required, the provision of such aids gives an added confidence in using the bath for therapeutic purposes.

For example, varicose veins can be alleviated by frequent

splashes or sprays with cold water. The cold water treatment can be continued for up to two minutes at a time. Tired eyes, sinusitis and frontal headaches can be subjected to the same cold splashing. Because body temperatures are generally lower in older people, febrile conditions do not arise so frequently. These can occur, however, and tepid sponging of the body and cold packs can be applied.

How to Apply a Wet Pack

The secret of applying a cold pack is to induce a moist-warmth condition which lowers temperature, reduces congestion and encourages elimination via the skin. The method, in older people, would be to apply a pack stretching from just under the armpits to the groin. This area would be enwrapped in a single piece of sheeting previously dipped into cold water and well wrung out. The wet sheeting would be covered with a similar-sized piece of dry blanketing or thick woollen garment, and both must be secured by safety pins. The patient would then immediately be put to bed with two hot water bottles to encourage a warm reaction.

The most practical manner in which to apply the pack is to pull back the bedclothes, place the dry covering (spread out) on the bed, then the wet sheet. The patient lies on the wet sheet, which is then pulled over close to the skin, quickly followed by the dry covering, which is then secured. The bedclothes are then drawn up and a hot water bottle placed at either side of the body.

The cold pack will be effective only if (a) the patient possesses the necessary vitality and (b) if the wet sheet is not too wet when applied. The latter is a frequent mistake and care should be taken to avoid this error. The cold pack should produce a sensation of warmth within a moment or two. If this fails, it must be removed. In normal circumstances, however, it should be pleasantly warm and remain on for anything from two to four hours. A tepid sponging should follow the cold pack.

The bedroom, like the bathroom, should be comfortably warm when being used for therapeutic purposes. However, since warmth is essential in age, all the house or flat should be at a fairly even but warm temperature.

Footbaths

Swollen and painful ankles frequently plague older people.

Relief and benefit to the general circulation can be gained by applying hot and cold footbaths to the feet and ankles. One bowl of hot water (as hot as can be tolerated) and one bowl of cold water are the only requirements. The feet should be immersed in the hot water for three minutes, then in the cold for half a minute to a minute and the process repeated three times, concluding with the cold application. Apart from supplying relief to the feet and ankles, this will also often relieve a headache.

Chronic ailments such as arthritis rarely cause a lack of appetite. Acute ailments, however, always produce a disinclination for food. This reduction in appetite is a natural instinct, since the body must devote energy to combating illness and not to the digestion and assimilation of unrequired food material. Loss of appetite in acute ailments is, therefore, a safety factor which should be respected. Providing the patient has warmth, rest and ample fluids, solid food can be avoided till the appetite and recovery from the acute symptoms are discernible.

Previous mention has been made of the reduction in body temperature which is a characteristic factor in age. Allowance has to be made for this variation. Additional care must be taken in allowing for a possible reduction in the inherent healing capacity of the body. After making all allowances, however, a fast or a semi-fast of a few days will create the conditions for recovery from many of the minor ailments which beset young and old. (A semi-fast consists of soft fruit, ample fruit juices and vegetable soups.) If bowel activity is interrupted, or a temporary costive state sets in during fasting then it would be advisable to give an enema of lukewarm water.

If strong objections are made to having an enema, a compromise must be insisted upon. This compromise would take the form of a herbal suppository or prune or raisin juice to which a teaspoon of agar-agar has been added. In addition, fruit jellies made from fruit and a seaweed preparation should be included in the diet.

Symptoms of Sluggish Bowel

At all times a close check should be kept on the bowel and kidney function of the older person. This is all the more essential when that person is temporarily confined to bed or movement is very restricted. A discoloured tongue, bad breath and poor state of the skin can be very indicative of poor bowel action. Lassitude, headaches and irritability are symptomatic of the same condition. However, since the memory of older people cannot be relied upon and there often exists an unnecessary fear of constipation, nothing can replace close observation and the adherence to a time schedule. The temporary insistence upon the use of a commode can be a useful guide to the natural function.

The same rule applies to the voiding of urine. Moreover, since diabetes is a fairly common complaint of the elderly, periodic testing of the urine is strongly advised. Confinement can make the use of a bed-pan essential in that it provides quick relief for the older person, eases his or her mind and allows checks to be made.

Aids to home nursing can be obtained or borrowed from most local authorities or voluntary associations. Assistance with nursing and domestic help is available to all elderly people in Britain. Schemes also exist in most districts for the older person not only to go on cheap, organized holidays, but also for recuperative treatment. Short spells away from the home surroundings can be a boon to both parties. When the older person is in reasonable health, these breaks should be insisted upon.

Obesity and over-eating must be avoided by the older person. Even in normal health there is a substantial reason for having one day per week on a very reduced diet, mainly of fruit and cottage cheese or yogurt. This gives the digestion a rest and creates the alkalinity essential to a good blood supply. On one day a month, a period of twenty-four hours without solid food (but with plenty of unsweetened fruit drinks, yeast extract or clear vegetable soup), would prevent many physical discomforts and increase resistance to disease. The drinks need not be confined to those mentioned. The tisanes or herbal teas provide beneficial changes in liquids. Lime blossom and maté tea, dandelion coffee and even rice water (from brown rice) and barley water can be welcome drinks. This is a variation of the weekly or fortnightly 'rest day'.

Fasting is a natural instinct which tends to be overlooked or frowned upon by anxious and misguided relatives. Even in the elderly, however, there are times when a short fast can avoid a great deal of future ill-health and speed recovery.

Importance of Home Care
Treatment for physical ailments is one aspect of healing which,

in the elderly, requires a great deal of patience, understanding and skill. So far as is humanly possible, it should all be carried out in the home atmosphere. What is equally important, however, is the instilling of confidence and boosting of morale which reduces the impact – and the incidence – of many minor ailments. To this end, especially with elderly ladies, the importance of the weekly 'hair-do', cosmetics and other aids to beauty should never be overlooked. To look well is an aid to feeling well.

Home care is infinitely preferable to institutional care. Older people must feel wanted and have the intimacy of the family circle. Failing that, the responsible person must be within easy reach and able to devote the necessary time for adequate care and attention. Less skilled home care – though the necessary skill can soon be acquired – provides the contentment, happiness and justification for living that institutions with more extensive facilities are unable to provide.

Few older people, even those with a very independent nature, will really opt for institutional care, no matter what efforts are made by these places to provide a personal atmosphere. In any case, a purely geriatric society lacks the stimuli which all people require. Occasional visits are no substitute for the home atmosphere, and a little home friction is better than boredom and lethargy. Complete unanimity can rarely be expected even when relationships are very close. Tolerance must spring from both sides, but occasional breaks, such as short holidays for the elderly, provide interludes which are absolutely essential. Fairness to the attendant, especially in home circumstances, is as important a therapeutic consideration as care for the older person.

CHAPTER THIRTEEN

SICK ROOM NURSING

In any case where extensive nursing and constant care is necessary the elderly invalid will, of course, be taken to a hospital or similar institution. There can, however, be numerous occasions when the geriatric is confined to bed for simple ailments which do not demand hospitalization. Furthermore, there are periods when the demand on hospital beds is so heavy that less serious cases have to either wait for admission or even be sent home to make way for more urgent admissions.

It is a recognized fact that old people survive better if they can be maintained in their surroundings and not subjected to the risk of possible cross-infection in hospital or the routine of normal hospital care. Old people like familiar surroundings, a sense of security, and the mass catering inevitable in large institutions can never approach that of the personal home. No matter what efforts are made in hospitals, most people – young or old – prefer to be in familiar surroundings.

The desire to be nursed at home is understandable, difficult though it may be to put into practice. Moreover, with the pressure on hospital space continuing unabated, it becomes almost a duty to avoid inessential admissions. Home nursing can and should be relieved by help from friends, relatives and a district nurse.

While it is not always feasible to choose the room in which an old person is to be nursed, it should, whenever possible, face south or south-west and be well ventilated but free from draughts. Too small a room can be claustrophobic, while a very large room (only encountered now in old buildings), can be equally disturbing. When the sick room is small, all unnecessary furniture should be removed.

Furniture for a Sick Room
The most important features of the sick room are a comfortable single bed with space for a helper on either side, a strong, but not too deep armchair, and a bedside trolley or small table. An adjustable cantilever table for meals, drinks and reading matter is a useful addition. A commode should be placed in a

convenient position or even be substituted for the armchair. Commodes can be obtained on loan by contacting the local authorities or health visitor. A strong, but not small, stool, is helpful when bathing the patient out of bed.

The mattress on the bed should be comfortable but firm and the bedclothing light but warm. The nature of the illness somewhat dictates the make-up of the bed. For most chest complaints it is necessary for the patient to be raised up on several pillows. If the old person has a history of hiatus hernia, the head of the bed has to be raised on blocks in addition to the extra pillows. Varicose veins and varicose ulcers demand that the foot of the bed be raised on blocks. Bed blocks should be a minimum of 6 and a maximum of 10 inches high.

Pressure from bedclothing can be avoided by using a wire cage between the sheets at the foot of the bed. As a temporary measure, however, a pillow may be utilized. It is essential to have some device for removing the weight of bed clothing if there is any wound on the legs or varicose ulcers are present.

Old people require warmth without weight, but there must be great care when they use electric blankets. Memory cannot be relied upon, sensations are not so sharp and there is a great danger of over-heating. While sleeping pills should be avoided as far as possible, there are times when it is difficult not to employ them, especially where there has been a history of drug-taking. Sleeping pills dull sensitivity and reaction to thermal stimuli; warning of the dangers of burning is absent or diminished. On the whole, covered hot water bottles are preferable to electric blankets. When sleeping pills or sedatives are being employed, electric blankets should certainly not be used.

Temperature in a Sick Room

Warmth is essential for the geriatric, but so is oxygen. The sick room, therefore, must be well ventilated. A screen can ward off any draught from the patient when a window is open. The temperature of the room should be kept between 65°-75°F. or 18.5°-24°C. Bold-type thermometers are now available and these are an improvement on the traditional wall thermometer, which can go unobserved.

High fever is unusual among the elderly, whose body temperatures tend to be lower than those of younger and more active age groups. The problem of hypothermia (or reduced body temperature) has been dealt with in Chapter Three. An old person can have a temperature of around 95°F. (the normal is 98.4°F.) without any apparent discomfort. Allowance, therefore, has to be made for this state of lowered temperature. Low-reading thermometers are now available and should be used when old people are sick.

Hygiene is, of course, one of the most important considerations, whether in the sick room or elsewhere. The utmost care has to be taken in keeping the patient and the room clean. By using bed-pans, urine bottles and commodes a great deal of work and effort can be saved. The patient must be kept as active as possible during nursing. Whenever practicable, therefore, even if some assistance is necessary, visits to the lavatory are preferable to using bed-aids or commodes. A commode is the next best thing to a lavatory, since it does involve a certain amount of activity.

A close watch has to be maintained on the bowel and bladder movements of the elderly invalid. This is more necessary when memory is unreliable or there is excessive modesty. Incontinence or involuntary bowel activity may possibly have to be taken into account. Disposable draw-sheets help to mitigate this problem. Mackintosh sheeting is also useful.

Recommended Method of Bed-changing

Bed-changing can be a performance unless carried out systematically. A recommended method of changing the bed without removing the sick person is to commence by removing the pillows. The patient is then turned upon one side and the soiled sheet is then rolled up lengthwise until the rolled sheet lies against the patient's back. The clean sheet is rolled up (also lengthwise) and one edge is tucked under the mattress on the vacant side and then unrolled until it lies adjacent to the roll of soiled sheet. The patient is then turned on his or her back and thence onto the clean sheet. The soiled sheet is pulled off the bed and the remainder of the clean sheet unrolled and tucked under the mattress.

The patient can remain covered by blankets and top sheet during the above process. A fresh draw-sheet or disposable sheeting can be introduced by the same method. Sometimes it is necessary to place a mackintosh sheet under the disposable or draw-sheet.

Hygiene demands particular attention to maintaining cleanliness of the patient and the bedclothes. But hygiene has other uses. It demands movement and changes in position and movement is one of the best safeguards against bed sores. If possible, it is in the interests of the patient for him or her to be escorted to the bathroom and given a warm (not hot) bath. This allows the bed to be changed and the sick room cleaned. The next alternative is to have the patient sitting in a chair and to be washed down in that position. Whichever method is employed it is important to remember that the patient should be kept warm. The minimum of exposure is the ideal aim.

Bathing the Patient in Bed
When it is necessary to bathe the patient in bed this is best achieved by doing one part of the body at a time. Commence with the face, then the arms, the front of the body and then the back. The patient, depending upon condition, should suffer the minimum exposure during bathing, though it will be necessary to remove different parts of the bed covering. When washing the back some assistance should be sought for lifting and turning. Conclude the bath by removing the lower section of bedclothing and bathe the legs and feet. Tepid water and gentle soap only should be used for the bathing and each part should be thoroughly dried after washing.

Bathing the patient takes care of hygiene, provides some movement and change of position and the effect of the water and the drying tones the skin and assists blood circulation. Any ulcerated area – namely a varicose ulcer – needs extremely gentle treatment. Nevertheless, the total effect of bathing is beneficial and reduces the time necessary for bed care. It should be emphasized, however, that the patient should be encouraged to go to the bathroom for bathing at the earliest possible moment, assisted, if necessary. Even when it is not feasible to walk to the bathroom, bathing should be accomplished sitting out of bed in a firm chair or on a strong stool.

Why Bed-sores Occur
Bed-sores are an indication of poor nursing, of previous poor nutrition and debilitated skin or neglect. Geriatrics who have been living alone and have spent too much time in bed or in sitting positions will frequently be found to have bed-sores prior to being taken under care. Anaemia and a protein, vitamin C and vitamin K deficiency must be considered when bed-sores are found or quickly develop. They can arise after one week of bed-

rest. The arch-enemy of bed-sores is activity. The excessive use of sedatives and sleeping pills, with the consequent reduction of normal stimuli and response, produces an inertia favourable to the production of pressure-sores.

Bed- (or pressure-) sores can arise from inactivity or from friction created by frequent involuntary movements or extreme restlessness. In such cases the limbs slide incessantly about in bed and set up the friction-sores. The vast majority of bed-sores, however, are the pressure-sores caused by unrelieved pressure while lying inert in bed.

The sites where bed-sores commonly form are, as could be expected, those places where the bones are visible through the skin. The skin is always in danger when there is pressure between an external object and the underlying bone. It is not surprising, therefore, that the dorsal spinal bones, the scapulae (shoulder blades), elbows, the sacrum and ischial tuberosities of the pelvis the great trochanters (bony prominences of the hips) and the heels should be the danger points for bed-sores. These are often displayed over the buttock area. If the patient tends to stay on one side, say the right, then it is the right elbow, buttock and heel which are at risk.

The weight of the patient, the relative frailty or lethargy, reduced sensation and poor nutrition, all have to be taken into account. But the prevention of bed-sores depends upon movement, cleanliness, the avoidance of wrinkles and crumbs in the sheets. A well-nourished skin will be more resistant to bed-sores. On the whole, however, the presence of such sores is a sign of inadequate nursing.

Good nursing means attention to the patient's needs in the way of bowel and bladder movements. It means bathing the patient with tepid water at least once a day and it means good attention to the state of the bed clothes and frequent changes in position.

Treatment of Sores
Sores should be treated by washing with soap and water and then by gentle massage around the area with sunflower oil or, if necessary, the application of a good herbal or other ointment. The sore area should be exposed to sunlight when possible and, failing that, to the fresh air. Exposure will assist the healing, but of course, care must be taken that the room is warm.

Recommended Diet

Never over-feed an invalid. Much depends upon the nature of the ailment. A temporary loss of appetite can actually be a safeguard. Providing sufficient *natural* fluids – clear vegetable soup with a yeast extract, unsweetened fruit juices, honey and water, are provided, life can be sustained and a recovery made from most simple ailments. Vitamin supplements: B12, Vitamins C and K, should be given with the drinks. Raw vegetable juices (an equal mixture of carrot, beetroot and apple) is recommended as a useful addition to the fluids, but the raw juice should be sipped.

Baby foods or a slippery elm food can usually be given on the second or third day of the illness, if they are desired. Beef teas have no food value in the true sense of the word, but invalid foods are available as a stop-gap till true appetite returns. Then a more normal diet can be supplied as recommended for geriatrics. Where some constipation has existed there should be a little emphasis on the laxative foods: prunes, soaked raisins, grated or cooked apple, spinach, mushrooms, beetroot, carrot, wholemeal bread and wholegrain cereals. If the bread and cereals are too coarse, molasses should be added to drinks and agar-agar sprinkled on food.

Old people can recover from minor illnesses just as well as younger members of the community. Care and attention is obviously necessary. What should be borne in mind, however, is that, while it may be a temptation to keep the elderly person safely tucked up in bed, this attitude can prolong the ailment and weaken the patient. Every encouragement should be given to the regaining of activity which, incidentally, is of value to both the patient and attendant. Also, while it may be irksome to administer to a sick and aged relative, there is also great satisfaction in seeing an old person recovering in his or her own home. Furthermore, an aged invalid usually recovers quicker when surrounded by relatives or friends.

CHAPTER FOURTEEN

THE 'DIFFICULT' GERIATRIC

The killer diseases – coronary thrombosis, cancer, and so on – take their toll. Lives are shortened by respiratory ailments – bronchitis, emphysema, bronchopneumonia. Stress and accidents reduce life expectancy. Poor nutrition and uncongenial environment can effectively reduce the life span by lowering the body's defences against disease, thus increasing the risk of early mortality. Obesity effectively limits life expectancy.

With the above in mind it is obvious that the people who reach old age have years of considerable resilience and tenacity behind them. Most must have been fortunate in their environment and hereditary influences. Few will have any history of continued abuse and most will have led contented and happy lives. This does not necessarily imply a high standard of living or above-average financial circumstances, though the latter does help. Thousands of old people have led simple and frugal lives, worked very hard – but on the whole enjoyed their work – and survive longer because of their frugality.

It must be said, however, that there are groups of old people and geriatrics who are difficult. There are many reasons why an old person can prove very exasperating to have in care. Some of the most difficult are not intentionally so; the reluctance to accept the limitations of age is easy to understand in a person who has been independent for so many years. Furthermore, those who have been able to command immediate attention can take an inordinately long time to adjust to changed circumstances. Independence, strength of will and physical resilience (or a life-long regard for physical fitness), are attributes of most people of advanced years. These attributes, however, do not always produce lovable characters!

In some, self-interest (not to be confused with self-indulgence), has been a dominating feature for decades. They have displayed a certain ruthlessness, a lack of acceptance of pain, probably because they possessed a low threshold of pain and little or no understanding of normal or lesser individuals. Such characters, in later years, can go one of two ways: either they become hypochondriac or persist in their dismissal of pain as representing nuisance-value only. Either way does not make for easy co-existence.

Motives for Independence

It is an unfortunate fact that the services of the relative, social worker or nurse are often unnecessarily delayed. Many old people, and even those not so old, will not accept advancing years and will make valiant efforts to assert their independence. Sometimes this is the outcome of vanity. There is nothing wrong with a modicum of vanity; it does imply efforts to maintain physical and mental effort. More often than not the independence is motivated by fear of being thought old and all it conjures up in the imagination of being dependent upon others – even close relatives. Too often, also, the efforts to remain independent are purely financial.

Many old people, fearful of security, pinch and save and deny themselves the very necessities of life. This hoarding for a 'rainy day' can become a fixation, even when there is no necessity for financial worry. Despite all that is available to older people in the way of pensions and other allowances, thousands of old people unnecessarily cut down on food, heat and the normal comforts of life and then present a real problem when they are no longer capable of self-care.

Apart from the 'creaking-gate' type, who so often seem to drain energy from other people, independence is a strong characteristic of most people of really old age. Even the 'creaking-gate' type often possess hidden reserves of energy which emerge when absolutely necessary.

The above characteristics, unfortunately, do not always make the task of looking after this group easy. It requires infinite patience and understanding even to make them accept that aid is necessary. Like a tired child who will not give in to sleep, the independent older person will resist help almost to the last. Furthermore, in the case of the old person who has acquired an almost miserly and hoarding attitude, it can be hard work to gain their confidence and trust. Old people can be extremely suspicious of married daughters or in-laws, as well as official or semi-official helpers.

It is when confined to bed for a while, or when in a state of semi-mobility, that the independent old person can be difficult indeed. Will-power has to be matched by will-power and ruthlessness has to be met with equal determination. The autonomous and slightly old person usually resents the help of strangers. However, no close relative should ever attempt the impossible by either helping an old person out of bed or onto a toilet or out of a bath single-handed. To do so invites the risk of injuring the helper's back; especially the lumbar spine and the shoulders. This applies even more with the difficult type under discussion.

Such old people can fight every inch of the way, insisting they do not need help and not relaxing. Others, even when strong characters, lack confidence in any help. Their fear of falling complicates the picture and makes assistance more difficult.

Equipment from Local Authorities

But the independence of many old people can be put to good use by selecting the correct kind of aid for their requirements. Even when such aids are only temporarily required, the old person should be encouraged to use them. Where home care is the order of the day, relatives or friends should not attempt anything which strains their physical capacity.

All unnecessary exertion should be avoided in the interests of both parties. Expert advice should be sought for the loan or acquisition of the particular aid required. Local authorities can, through various agencies, provide equipment and aids which ease home nursing and, in the case of the independent old person, increase that independence.

This is particularly important when, after a period of confinement which has reduced strength and mobility, such aids are necessary. There may initially be some resistance to adopting aids such as zimmers, but perseverance and the appeal to their independence eventually wins the day.

Difficult old people will usually have sharply defined ideas about food. With the passage of years, however, and the corresponding decline in appetite, this can be less of a problem than procuring co-operation in other directions. Determined geriatrics are, on the whole, less food conscious than most. It is, indeed, usually one of the reasons why they have reached their mature years.

Vitamin and Mineral Supplements

Simple, attractive meals reduce tendencies to indigestion, flatulence and constipation. Avoiding these disturbances can minimize irritability in the elderly. Vitamin and mineral supplements are usually necessary for all old people and some cajoling may be necessary to make the very independent type accept the supplements. Furthermore, it is essential to actually witness the taking of the supplements. Apart from failing memory (a fact often strenuously denied by the independent geriatric), there can be a question of deliberate deception to avoid taking them.

Caring for old people can be a hard task; so much depends upon the character of the geriatric involved. Some determined old people have probably never really been lovable characters, but they are usually in the minority. It is necessary to understand, appreciate and tolerate the continued fight for independence and, wherever possible, turn it to advantage.

CHAPTER FIFTEEN

RETIREMENT AND MOVING

On retirement, the lucky people are those who can, when asked how retirement suits them, truthfully say 'I don't know how I found time to work!' Such an answer denotes a zest for life and wide interests. It is, too, almost as good an assurance as possible that a healthy old age is either reached or will be attained.

There is no need to envy such people – it is within reach of all. In any case, retirement at 60 or even 65 should leave years and years of active existence, even to the point of taking further but less arduous occupation. The trend is towards earlier and earlier retirement and, at the executive and middle-management level, there are tentative moves towards retirement at 50. One side-effect of such early retirement would be to stimulate the demand for re-training for other work. Providing that adequate re-training facilities are available and offer sufficient scope for talent, earlier retirement can be an advantage. It is easier to re-train and adjust at 50 than it is at 60 or 65 and the earlier age leaves more time for activity in the new occupation.

Self-employed people do, in any case, often continue long after normal retiring age. The delayed retirement age for the self-employed is usually dictated by economics. The failure to acquire sufficient capital to ensure early or normal retirement, however, is often a blessing in disguise. Providing working hours and responsibility can be progressively reduced as age increases, there is every inducement and advantage – physically and financially – in delaying retirement.

Outside Interests
The very worst thing is to retire with no outside interests or hobbies and no idea what to do. For the average married woman, the only problem about retirement is either financial, in having to maintain the household on a reduced income or a change in routine with the husband at home. Even this change requires some time for adjustment on both sides. It can, indeed, call for such a complete change in household routine that the advantages of retirement can be questioned by the wife!

For many people, particularly the stay-at-home wife, the

novelty of retirement may soon wear thin. This is especially the case when the retired man spends too much time sitting around in the house, not knowing what to do. Retirement requires careful thought and planning to avert possible mutual frustration and exasperation. It also calls for diplomacy on both sides till a real adjustment to the change in position, income and routine is established. One of the surest ways of creating a happy retired marital life is for both parties to have and continue with their own interests. It is not necessary for these interests to coincide – in practice this is not usual in any event – but it is essential for both sides to continue the outside interests they normally pursue as long as possible.

Before retirement, thought should be given as to what hobbies or mental and physical reactions should be adopted. Some firms do give pre-retirement advice and training and a great deal more is required to be achieved in this direction. On average, however, very little is done in this respect despite the fact that future mental and physical health will be governed by maintaining mental and physical agility. In these more enlightened days and with the growth in the numbers of senior citizens, even more resources will have to be placed at the disposal of the elderly.

Fortunately, there are many associations and bodies which help people in retirement and many are not fully used. Such services should not be spurned; they can lead to a fuller social life. It is a great mistake, however, to rely entirely upon other people. The greatest benefit is by helping oneself. In other words, it is more important to be healthy, thereby reducing the toll on the health and social services and being an asset to the community, instead of a liability. Although society must take its share of responsibility, the onus is still largely on the individual. It is, after all, his life and his future which is at stake. Whether or not it is going to be a happy and contented future depends upon past care and past history.

Retirement presents many problems and decisions. Uppermost, and especially with those living in industrial regions with their special problems of pollution, is the problem of uprooting and moving to more salubrious surroundings or a drier and sunnier region. This region in Britain, as we have seen, is usually the south-east of England, where a preponderance and artificial grouping of aged people already exists. The wealthier can venture abroad, or even elect to live abroad in the winter months.

For older people, the policy of a winter holiday is, on the whole, preferable to a summer vacation. But to venture abroad to seek the sun in winter just for one or two weeks can be disastrous. Southern Europe may be milder and sunnier than northern climes, but winter is still winter and it can rain every day practically for two weeks or more. Only well-established areas – South Africa, Florida and other southern latitudes – can practically guarantee 'summer-in-winter'.

Short Winter Holidays

Depending upon financial standing and physical capacity, short winter holidays can be useful. The best procedure, however, is to get away, not for two weeks, but for six to eight weeks. During that time many of the rigours of northern climates can be eluded, there is a real chance of some sunny weather and, at very least, the rain is not so cold and depressing. Long winter holidays are not so impracticable. The idea of such holidays is already flourishing and will continue to do so. Winter holidays of this type are, after all, merely an extension of normal tourist traffic geared to the retired population. As such, they become practical propositions which only require investigation to prove their worth. Protracted winter holidays can even reduce the necessity for moving house.

Those who can and wish to move should give it a great deal of thought. Assuming that one or two specific districts have been selected, then no choice should be made until a fair amount of time has been spent in each district. It is wise to become really acquainted with the locality and its amenities. A hill, which may present no problem at 65 or 70 can be a severe obstacle to shopping expeditions or walking in later years. A flight of steps can present a future hazard. Public transport is another question. A car may not always be available; even a driving licence may have to be surrendered! These considerations are not pessimistic musings; they are hard realistic facts.

On retirement, a move may be advisable for several reasons: social, economic, health and convenience. In the normal run of events sons and daughters have married and left the family home and there is little purpose in maintaining an establishment which is in excess of requirements. In many cases the garden is too large, too expensive to maintain and a burden rather than a pleasure. On the other hand, even the thought of parting with cherished furniture or items gathered over the years involves a fearful wrench. Moving, in fact, is a process which, ideally, should be a gradual transition. To this end it is better to part with some objects gradually, and preferably to where they are appreciated!

Planning a Retirement Home

If it is found desirable to seek a home for retirement, then the decision, while it should never be hasty, should not be delayed to the extent that physical and mental resources are over-taxed when accomplishing it. Moving means a complete rearrangement of life, routine and, for the first few weeks, not a little physical effort. Even moving a relatively short distance can create a gulf between friends and acquaintances. This has also to be taken into serious account.

Excessive delay can reduce the capacity to make new social contacts. Time, unfortunately, often makes the older person more and more dependent upon their own resources, just when they require that extra assistance. People, old and young, must be wanted and all need both to give help and receive it. Many older people find both things less easy, unless the habit and conditions are right. With reduced energy and adaptability, which does come from age, the retirement home can become a very lonesome place if undue delay reduces the propensity for making contacts.

Many retired people bitterly regret moving. A lot of the regret could be avoided if real preparation, time and thought had been given to the subject. Better climatic conditions do not always balance the loss of associates and the frequent visits of close relations, especially children and grandchildren. If a move is made, therefore, it should be with a determination to seek other friendly outlets and the pursuit of some hobby or recreation.

Three Indispensable Considerations

Contact, communication and care. These are the three things which must be kept very much in mind when contemplating any retirement move. All three are indispensable in the later stages of life. Furthermore, future happiness or otherwise can be involved if distance reduces the opportunity for relatives and friends to provide contact, communication and care. Despite establishing new contacts and forging a new way of life, old acquaintanceships die hard and become more valuable with the passing of time. In many ways, therefore, it can be an advantage for the older person not to move, but to find an escape in longer holidays, especially in the winter.

Few people can afford to have a lengthy stay in any district chosen for retirement. A good alternative, therefore, once an area is more or less settled upon, is to spend a few days there at different periods of the year, to see if it is still attractive in all the seasons. Winter is vastly different from summer! Also, before buying or renting a flat, house or bungalow, contact the local authorities and check what development plans are scheduled for the locality. Some nasty surprises can be avoided by persistent enquiry! Some local authorities, too, make better provision for senior citizens than others. A little comparison with different areas is a prudent measure.

Homes for the really elderly or slightly infirm require a great deal of thought. Everything possible should be done to facilitate ease of movement, unnecessary bending and reaching, sharp corners, dim passages and heavy doors. Handles of all furniture, doors, taps, and so on, should be easy to grip and turn. Windows should open easily and while some furniture (beds, for example), can be placed on casters, movement of such furniture should not be too free. Accidents can happen from attempting to sit on beds or chairs which shift with the slightest move and cause a fall. Safety, convenience and warmth are vital to the older person.

Adapting the Retirement Home

A fit older person can adapt the retirement home. Few houses or flats contain the fittings which may be necessary in later life. One of the advantages of not leaving the move to an age where physical effort and mental energy are reduced is that the home can be gradually altered to meet the changing needs.

Local authorities and various associations can assist with fixing aids in the home for the elderly and disabled. Advice, if not outright assistance, can be obtained from such sources. Many accidents can be prevented by a little forethought in rendering the home safe. Accidents in the home are more serious to the elderly than to any section of the public. The provision of handrails in bathroom and lavatory, on both sides of steps or staircases and in any long passage, are often vital for safe movement.

On average, the person who lives to an advanced age is made of sterner stuff and is not easily intimidated by minor setbacks. Even so, a fall from imbalance can be a serious blow to confidence. In the seventies, balance is often less efficient. When degenerative changes have taken a heavier toll, or posture, obesity or arterial disease have an adverse influence on balance, aids to safety in movement are essential. Slight disabilities from arthritic changes, for instance, can limit mobility and balance, especially when such changes affect the hips and knees. Movement is absolutely essential to life. The provision of safety rails and bars should not be left too late.

Simple Precautions
It is generally conceded that life can never be equal. The less active and able stage can be reached in one partner before the other. Physical movements can be more difficult in the husband or wife, due to earlier skeletal or muscular degeneration or imbalance in that person and the necessity for aids to mobility and safety rarely coincide. Simple precautions, taken when physical powers and energy are available, are better than the risk of serious accident and the sudden realization that such aids are necessary.

The more active partner – whether husband or wife – should encourage the addition of safety aids in the home, no matter what his or her personal feelings on the subject may be and despite the fact that such aids are totally unnecessary for the other partner. Many such aids will undoubtedly have to be diplomatically installed, since the last impression that should be given to any person is that activity should be limited. The aim of safety aids should be to encourage and not discourage mobility.

Provision for age should not be left to insurance and pension schemes only. Assurance for health in old age and the chronological age when a person feels old, is basically a question of past history and the care or disregard of basic health laws. Nature has a simplicity which is often forgotten by sophisticated societies. We are just beginning to learn, in this polluted age, that nature cannot be ignored.

People are living longer; it is therefore necessary that they should be healthier. There is no point in age if life is just one set of complications, difficulties and physical disability. Unless the true standard of health is raised there can be vast numbers of people who consume a disproportionate share of the resources and activities of the younger section. Prevention of disability, the curtailment of degeneration and a reduction in accidents are essential to the national economy. New approaches and thinking are required on the subject of age, health and the prevention of degenerative diseases. These approaches should spring from official, as well as private, sources.

CONCLUSION

The most difficult task is to predict future trends. All that is really possible is to hazard an intelligent guess. There is no doubt that people are living longer – but can the process go on? People who are now past the 75 age group were born in tougher times; where cars were few and far between, where more physical effort was demanded in work; where food (though possibly less abundant) contained more *real* nutriment; where pollution was less advanced and where more discipline was demanded.

Affluence and a higher standard of living has not produced more contentment or eased many burdens. On the contrary, increased standards of living have increased the hazards of life, even if only to the extent that few people, for instance, go through life without being involved in a traffic accident. For millions of people the decline in 'job satisfaction' makes it all the more imperative that retirement years should at least hold out more hope.

Millions of people are dissatisfied with modern life. Many of these have only vague ideas as to the cause of their dissatisfaction and are unable to pinpoint the actual reasons. A large proportion of them – because of nutritional deficiencies created by mass catering and modern methods of food cultivation and preparation – have not really experienced the art of living. They are neither healthy nor basically unhealthy, but exist in a border-line state where correct nutrition could immensely improve their health or a serious illness completely undermine it, especially if the latter involves potent drug treatment. Ignorance and apathy frequently dictate the course and these are the enemies of future health and happiness.

Drug-taking
In the nineteen-hundreds few people took sleeping pills or drugs for stimulation. Drug-taking was not only on a much reduced scale – the drugs were less toxic and had fewer side-effects. These days, thousands of people take drugs because 'I feel a headache is coming on' or 'Just in case I can't sleep'. Common though it is,

such an attitude brooks ill for future development and health. Drug-taking is not confined to adults; there are even aspirins for children! The earlier a person starts taking drugs, the longer the eventual past history of drug-taking will be and the accumulated toxic effects on the body must be correspondingly greater.

What is urgently required, while the opportunities still exist, is a comparative research into the stamina, vitality and *absolute* health of the person born in the 1900s, and 1930s and the 1960s. A great many factors would have to be borne in mind: hygiene, nutrition, change in diseases, environment, etc. Has the younger person of today less stamina or less *absolute* health than his forebears? It is possible that he has, yet he could live longer on a reduced level of health and be more of a charge on the community. There are enormous implications in this prospect.

Such research should ignore, as the normal person should, the fact that world records in athletics are constantly being broken. The breaking of such records only proves what scientific training (and sometimes the use of drugs), can achieve. Turning a human being into a swimming or running machine, magnificent though this may be, has little significance for the ordinary person and his ability to live a longer and healthier life. Because a few people can prove vastly superior to their ancestors on the athletic field is not proof of a higher general standard. Superior talent in athletics does not infer a longer span of life. On the contrary, by constantly burning up reserves of energy in the pursuit of athletic prowess, the chances of a healthy longevity could be curtailed.

The question uppermost is that of the ultimate effect of 'soft' sophisticated and artificial living to which most people are now subject. Are we sufficiently aware of the long-term effects and the prospects on future ageing?

Ethical Problems

What does raise a very large ethical problem is whether, after a severe or incurable illness when the person is either a cripple or severely handicapped or even senile or approaching senility, the relatives or friends can be fairly asked to shoulder the burden of nursing. It also raises the problem that life-saving antibiotics and surgery often save lives and prolong what has become a merely vegetable existence. The instinct to preserve life and the instinct to survive are, fortunately, ever present. Thus, while many useful lives can be saved by resorting to drugs at the crucial moment, many survive for months or even years more when nature would have decreed otherwise. There are, in fact, insufficient institutions to cater for this problem.

Sensational reports about euthanasia do nothing to mollify the problem of the aged. An older person must feel wanted to justify his or her existence. Careless conjecture can only cause apprehension and unnecessary fears. The trend, however, is for less and less home care. If any inducement to maintain personal health exists, it should be for this reason alone.

Many people of advanced age require minimal assistance only. Most people who reach advanced ages retain an independent spirit and a surprising degree of resilience. This is one of the reasons they have reached advanced age. Thousands more suffer from degenerative arthritis, arterio-sclerosis and other degenerative changes but still lead active, if limited, lives.

Assistance an Entitlement

Should daughters or sons devote a great part of their life and resources to the care of elderly parents? What used to be accepted as a normal duty is now questioned, despite increased pensions, allowances and financial assistance. But few people like hospitals and institutions, and the risk of infection at home is far less than in such places. Only in the last resort, or in an emergency, therefore, should aged and sick people be sent away. This does, of course, involve relatives or friends in the task of caring for old people. Circumstances will vary, but home care for the aged should never be left to one person alone. Full use should be made of all the help – official and unofficial – that can be obtained. Assistance in the care of the elderly is a recognized entitlement. Attendance allowances for the aged are available in the United Kingdom. The same rule applies for giving hard-pressed helpers a respite from catering for the geriatric by the old person having occasional 'rests' in the institutions and homes provided for the purpose. It is necessary for the individual who becomes responsible for an aged parent or relative to make full enquiries to ensure that the appropriate assistance is forthcoming.

Fear of Accidents

The really old – again, no matter what age – can be querulous, repetitive and fearsome to the point of exasperation. They can also be suspicious, intolerant and completely forgetful of time. There is, too, if they are active, the constant fear of imbalance causing accidents. They can be alarming, too, in that very minor strokes or slight and temporary occlusions of the brain can cause black-outs or mental confusion. There is also the ever-present problem of slight (or even severe) incontinence, which can be an embarrassment to the sensitive older person and a burden to those responsible for them. None of this makes home care easy.

The problems of advanced age are not insoluble. Time, patience, kindness and understanding is required to maintain an elderly infirm parent at home, and this should be shared. Too frequently it is left to one person alone. If that person is a married daughter with children of her own it can create serious domestic problems. A son, asking his wife to care for his elderly mother, can also be placed in a quandary. Fortunate people often solve the problem by providing a small separate flat in their home.

The effect on children when an aged parent is part of the household depends entirely upon the characteristics of the people involved. Children are great mimics and they can also be jealous. Providing, however, that children are not neglected because of the time involved in looking after an old person, they accept the situation as normal and even assist where they can. Most children are sympathetic to aged grandparents and they can be an influence for good. Furthermore, grandparents and even great-grandparents can be very useful in helping young children and derive much pleasure in that task. Older people should not be excluded from the joys of the family circle, nor must their contribution be disdained. Retirement and advanced age can and should be a happy period of life and close proximity with the family keeps many an old person alert and healthy.

Avoiding Immobility

The mistake in caring for the elderly at home is the tendency to keep the old person in bed or safely ensconced in a chair. This immobility inevitably leads to stagnation, bed sores and a rapid deterioration in the physical condition. Even when in bed, the old person should be encouraged to move about and exercise the limbs The minimum of bed and chair rest is essential to life. The older person, in fact, needs encouragement to move around and exercise the limbs to avoid stiffness of joints and weak muscles. Fatigue should be the criterion of resting. Once fatigue has set in, then rest should be taken. Frequent movement, interspersed with periods of resting, therefore, should be the aim. Obesity must always be avoided. Retention of fluid and flatulence can create a false impression of obesity, but both effects are reduced when mobility is retained.

Enforcing Restricted Diet

There can be severe protestations and difficulties when attempts are made to alter the diet and insist on movement in an attempt to improve the health of an older person. Sometimes it is better not to reason. Providing the food is served in an attractive manner, the restricted diet for the older person should be enforced. It can avoid some of the digestive troubles – especially flatulence – which plague older people and it can restore the nutritional imbalance from which they probably suffer, or have suffered.

Movement is vital, even when there is opposition from the person concerned. The opposition can arise from fear of moving painful joints and the dread of falls from imbalance. The provision of safety aids, walking appliances, bars, and so on, plus actual physical help are often necessary if mobility is to be maintained. Tact, kindness, tolerance and firmness have to be combined to encourage confidence and retain as much mobility as possible.

Looking after ageing parents can raise many problems. There are numerous temptations to shed the responsibility. In a changing age this factor must be recognized. This should increase the determination to avoid the pitfalls of early degeneration by adopting enlightened methods of living. Healthy old age, no matter what the chronological age, is a consequence of healthy living.

Natural Laws of Living

Thousands of people in their 80s and 90s have proved to their satisfaction that, when more natural laws of living are obeyed the result is a happy, contented and physically fit old age. Many, in fact, have proved that illnesses in their earlier years have been a blessing in disguise because, during the illness, he or she learnt the value of health and how to look after it by more attention to natural laws.

Old at 50 – young at 80? The answer to this problem is within the reach of everyone and it is every person's duty to find it. Years of useful work, effort and thought for other people demand some compensation in later life. However, when more attention is paid to a more natural way of life a great deal of compensation can be found in living a longer and more active life, free from many of the accepted degenerative symptoms. The other and equally important compensation is that of retaining independence. When, however, assistance is required it should be freely given and graciously accepted. *Duty* is the personal element in doing everything possible during earlier years to prevent, delay and minimize the degeneration of age. But duty brings enjoyment of good health and is a sound investment for future years. Age can and should produce its own compensation and the last stages of life should not be feared and endured – they should be enjoyed, providing this enjoyment is first an individual responsibility, then the responsibility of relatives, friends and the State. It is a task no one should shirk.

Threat of Loneliness
The passing of years produces the growing threat of loneliness to the elderly. Each month, each year, sees the demise of a friend, relative or other contemporary. Isolation and the disappearance of familiar faces and contacts all come at a time when it is less easy to withstand shock and accept change. The fact that there may be a perfect understanding of the inevitability that life must end some time and that age will produce its toll on contemporaries does not necessarily ease the sense of loss. It certainly does nothing to reduce the reminder that age has its limitations.

The essentials of a happy retirement (apart from health) are a sense of security, the reduction of loneliness and the necessity to feel wanted. Associations and organizations for the old can minimize the threats, shocks and disadvantages incumbent upon age. But the best organization cannot replace the family unit. It is this factor which must be kept very much in mind by younger sections of the community. That some pecuniary gain may ensue from the demise of an elderly relative should never colour the approach to the problem. This latter factor must obviously intrude upon the mind of most people; material matters are not that easily dismissed. What is important, however, is that the aged person should enjoy the years remaining to him or her without undue worry; without feeling a burden and without sensing that a cash value is placed upon them. Old people have human rights and human feelings – common humanity dictates a respect for these qualities.

The problems of the aged are not insoluble. More thought in earlier years could drastically reduce those problems. There is a special need to eliminate the part played by degenerative diseases in later life. In this direction alone a vital contribution can be made to human happiness and economy. The extent of this contribution depends upon individual effort, but, in making this effort, the gain, both personal and social, is highly satisfactory.

INDEX